GW01557942

Southern Africa's Beautiful Deserts

The Big Picture

Photography by
HEINRICH VAN DEN BERG
PHILIP VAN DEN BERG
INGRID VAN DEN BERG

Text by
GORDON MACLEAN
CHERIE MACLEAN

Published by
HPH Publishing

Life on Earth cannot exist without water, yet deserts abound with life. An astonishing diversity of animals and plants have evolved extraordinary and often bizarre ways of surviving in the desert. Where rainfall is scarce and erratic, these organisms cannot always rely on it for biological events, such as breeding, and have had to adapt in other ways.

The region designated in this book as 'desert' includes the Namib, the Succulent Karoo, the Nama Karoo and the Arid Savanna. The last-mentioned is also called the Kalahari and is the more arid part of the southern African savanna, covering about 46% of southern Africa. These are the main so-called 'thirstland' divisions of the arid and semi-arid parts of southern Africa. Arid regions are defined as those with an average annual rainfall of less than 250 millimetres; semi-arid regions have average annual rainfalls of between 250 and 500 millimetres. A true desert has little or no rain in most years and would be classed as 'arid' or even 'extremely arid'.

The main climatic features of deserts are relatively low and unpredictable rainfall combined with high daytime temperatures in summer, frequently above 45° C, and very cold night-time temperatures in winter, often as low as −15° C, with quite severe frost. This results in sparse vegetation, so that the arid zone is characterized visually largely by the colours and textures of its soil types, be they sand, gravel or rock.

The desert and semi-desert areas of southern Africa stretch from just north of the major cities of Cape Town and Port Elizabeth on the southern coast of South Africa, northwards for about 2 400 kilometres in a broad band of between 700 and 1 200 kilometres from west to east and extend into Botswana and Namibia. This band then tapers off northwestwards until it peters out in southwestern Angola at about the latitude of Lobito. It measures about 1.6 million square kilometres – an area bigger than the combined land surfaces of France, Spain, Germany and the United Kingdom. More than half of South Africa and Botswana, about two-thirds of Namibia, and a small part of Angola fall within this arid region.

Deserts are surprisingly variable. Even in one type of desert habitat, such as the Namib, one may find an inland sea of towering sand dunes glowing in pink and gold with blinding white claypans in between, or one may cross endless gravel plains of pale greyish-mauve, interrupted by inselbergs of stark black or dark brown rock. Across these vast areas are several dry watercourses etched into the desert floor and embroidered with a line of green acacia and ebony trees along each bank.

The Kalahari presents a rather different picture. It is characterized by salmon-orange sand dunes covered mostly by a mixture of coarse grass, low shrubs and sparse thornveld – the arid savanna. The sand overlies a layer of fairly hard limestone called calcrete which is exposed here and there by the prevailing winds to produce larger or smaller areas of whitish stony ground. The dunes and the calcrete have their own special flora and fauna.

And then there is the Nama Karoo, which is really two separate and somewhat different types of semi-desert. The Great Karoo lies north of the Grootswartberge, part of the Cape Fold Mountains; it has a mainly summer rainfall in its eastern reaches and merges into a mainly winter-rainfall stretch of Succulent Karoo in the west. The Little Karoo lies south of this range of mountains, sandwiched between it and the Langeberg and Langkloofberg ranges nearer the coast; its rain falls mainly in winter, so that its vegetation shares many features with that of the Succulent Karoo. All these mountains form a barrier to the moist air moving inland and northwards from the Indian Ocean and contribute to the aridity of the Karoo.

Of all the world's arid places, the Namib, the Succulent Desert, the Nama Karoo and the Kalahari of southern Africa are biologically the most diverse. They include some of the most important conservation areas in the region, from small nature reserves like Vrolijkheid and the Karoo Botanical Garden in the southwest, Beaverlac Nature Reserve and the Tanqua-Karoo National Park further north, to the more extensive regions like the Karoo, Richtersveld, Kgalagadi Transfrontier and Central Kalahari National Parks, in South Africa and Botswana. Namibia includes extremely important parks like Fish River Canyon, Namib-Naukluft, Skeleton Coast and Etosha – which are among the largest conservation areas in the world.

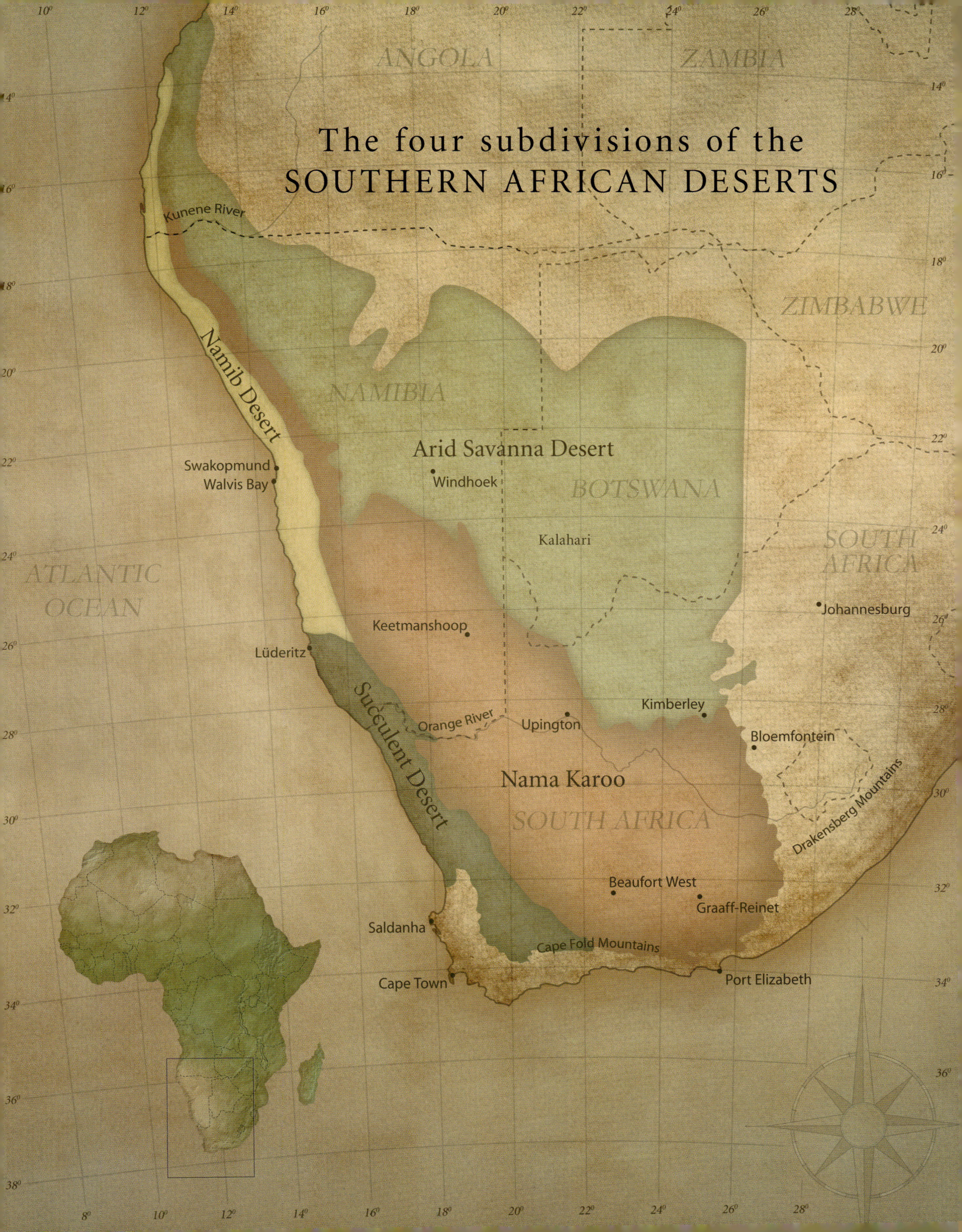

The four subdivisions of the
SOUTHERN AFRICAN DESERTS

ANGOLA

ZAMBIA

Kunene River

ZIMBABWE

NAMIBIA

Namib Desert

Arid Savanna Desert

Swakopmund
Walvis Bay

Windhoek

BOTSWANA

Kalahari

ATLANTIC
OCEAN

SOUTH
AFRICA

Keetmanshoop

Johannesburg

Lüderitz

Succulent Desert

Orange River

Upington

Kimberley

Bloemfontein

Nama Karoo

SOUTH AFRICA

Drakensberg Mountains

Beaufort West

Graaff-Reinet

Saldanha

Cape Fold Mountains

Cape Town

Port Elizabeth

The northward-flowing Benguela Current in the Atlantic Ocean washes the Namib Desert along southern Africa's west coast. Relatively warm surface seawater is deflected seawards by the rotation of the earth, resulting in upwelling of deeper, colder layers of nutrient-rich water against the land, thus making the coastal waters one of the richest fishing grounds in the world. The fish provide food for thousands of marine mammals and birds such as Cape Cormorants (previous spread), Cape Fur Seals (above) and Cape Gannets (opposite).

Namib Desert

Arid Savanna

Nama Karoo

Succulent Desert

NAMIB DESERT

The Namib Desert is the western extremity of a huge arid to semi-arid region (including the Kalahari and Karoo), which lies in the rain shadow of the eastern and southern escarpments – the Eastern Highlands of Zimbabwe, the Drakensberg and the Cape Fold Mountains. This desert stretches from just south of the Orange River in a narrow strip, mostly less than 150 kilometres wide, for about 2 000 kilometres to southern Angola.

There can be few more dramatic contrasts than that between the cold Benguela Current of the Atlantic Ocean and the hot Namib Desert along the coast of Namibia. The Benguela Current is one of the biologically richest marine habitats on Earth, and is all water! The Namib is one of the harshest deserts on earth and is almost completely devoid of surface water; it therefore also has very few living things compared with the adjacent sea. Indeed the very presence of the cold seawater washing the Namib edge increases the desert's aridity. How does this happen?

Along its western edge the Namib receives an almost nightly invasion of fog from the Atlantic Ocean, extending 60 kilometres or more towards its eastern edge along the escarpment formed by the Naukluft and other mountain ranges. This fog, which amounts to the equivalent of about 50 millimetres of rain a year, rises from the sea into the relatively cooler night air, disperses inland and evaporates as the morning sun warms the air. The warm air above the fog acts as a lid or inversion layer and prevents the formation of rain clouds, thereby increasing the aridity of the desert.

Temperatures across the Namib from the coast to its inland edge vary considerably. Generally the coastal strip is cool to mild because of the cold ocean and the resulting fog; its relatively high humidity has allowed a wonderful array of lichens to evolve. In places they provide characteristic colours to the desert floor – black, white or orange. Daytime temperatures increase inland, and day-night variations are more extreme, especially beyond the influence of the nightly fog.

Like any other desert, the Namib presents different faces. In the south it merges with the Succulent Karoo with its winter rainfall and its own special life forms. In the north the scanty rain falls mainly in summer, and its plants and animals differ accordingly.

Much of the Namib is covered with sand dunes of different colours and shapes, depending on the source of the sand and the nature of the prevailing winds. The dunes move according to the force and direction of the wind. The windward side is a rather gentle slope of relatively firm sand rising from the desert floor, to a crest that falls away as a slipface on the leeward side. Interestingly it is this unstable slipface which harbours most of the living animals – beetles and other insects, spiders, golden moles, lizards and snakes.

Where the sand is less shifting on the windward side burrowing mammals like gerbils prefer to live. Here also grow the sparse clumps of coarse dune grass, *Stipagrostis sabulicola*. These clumps form 'islands' that provide microhabitats for many Namib animals, including the Dune Lark, which occurs nowhere else in the world. Indeed, almost every animal and plant found in the Namib, especially in the fog zone, is endemic to the region. Since the Namib is such an important 'centre of endemism' its conservation is vital.

The winds that sculpt the sand also deliver food to the bottom of the Namib's food chain in the form of dry grass and other material from inland. This and the fog are the very basis of survival for plants and animals in this remarkable region: the dry wind-blown plant material absorbs moisture from the fog at night; large animals like antelopes and ostriches eat this and thereby obtain a significant amount of both water and nourishment. Reptiles and some insects drink the moisture that condenses on their bodies; other insects as well as small mammals drink the water formed by the fog as it condenses on the sand. These animals in turn provide food for predatory birds, lizards and snakes. And so a food chain is perpetuated.

The Namib shows another face in the extensive gravel plains and the gravelly troughs between the dunes. Some of these troughs or 'valleys' are a kilometre or more wide. The gravel flats further inland form a somewhat stonier desert pavement and have very different fauna and flora from those in the dune sea. They tend to be pale pinkish or greyish-mauve in colour. Animals that inhabit these plains are camouflaged in similar pale colours – for example Rüppell's Korhaan and Gray's Lark among the birds. Even further inland you will find rough stony ground that merges with the brown rocky foothills of the escarpment.

More or less isolated mountains (inselbergs) or low hills of rock that dot the Namib here and there create some relief to the eye from the glare of the sand and gravel. These features occur in a variety of colours, depending on their geology, ranging from black through brown, to pink and white. Those that occur in the fog belt are especially important as sites of condensation on their hard surfaces, because enough water may even run off them to help the germination of seeds and the survival of plants that exist at their bases. Indeed the fog will condense on the leaves and stems of the plants themselves; such droplets may fall to the ground or in some cases may even be absorbed directly by the leaves of certain succulent plants.

Of all the watercourses that run from east to west across the Namib Desert, only two take the form of perennial rivers – the Orange in the south and the Kunene in the north. Because of their perennial flow and the gallery forest of trees that line much of their banks, they cannot be considered part of the 'desert' environment. However, several major dry river courses wend their way across the Namib, some of which, such as the Kuiseb, have an almost permanent flow of water under the sand that forms their beds. They may also have some fairly impressive gallery forests of Ana, Cape Ebony and Mustard Trees, even deep into the desert proper.

Such watercourses provide special conditions, often including free water, and are inhabited by species of plants and animals that are not strictly desert-adapted. Antelopes and zebras may dig for water in the dry riverbed, sometimes finding it as little as a metre from the surface. There are even African Elephants and giraffes in the northern Namib, an area known as the Kaokoveld, which make good use of these riverine habitats for food and water.

One of the actions of these rivers is to prevent the sand sea from migrating northward under the influence of the prevailing winds, because, when they flow upcountry after good rains, the sand that has blown into their paths gets washed downstream. This is why dunes occur to the south of most of these rivers, and gravel plains to the north. Again the Kuiseb is the most typical example of such a system. It was the presence

of occasional waterholes in the Kuiseb valley that allowed the German geologists Hermann Korn and Henno Martin to survive their self-imposed exile of nearly two years during the Second World War.

Previous spread
Much of the Namib Desert is covered with sand dunes that move according to the force and direction of the wind. In years of good rainfall, wide gravel plains between the dunes may be covered with grass. Low hills of rock that dot the Namib here and there are important sites of condensation of nocturnal fog, which helps the germination and survival of plants that grow at their bases.

The colouring and markings of Péringuey's Adder resemble the wind-blown sand that is its home on the coast of Namibia. While waiting for lizards to come within striking distance, it conceals itself in the sand, leaving exposed only its tail tip and its eyes, which are on top of its flat head. Sometimes it moves its tail tip to attract prey.

Being a small snake (20-25 centimetres), with mild venom, Péringuey's Adder is endangered by over-collecting for the pet trade. Known also as a 'sidewinder', the adder moves smoothly over the sand by looping its body sideways, leaving a track of parallel S-shaped grooves. It can even scale 45° slopes of loose sand in this way.

Geckos are a family of lizards distinguished by a bizarre variety of eyes and feet. The Web-footed Gecko's large eyes are an indication of its nocturnal habits; it emerges from its tunnel in the sand at sunset to feed on small insects and spiders. Webbed toes on its front and back feet help to distribute its weight on the sand and stop that sinking feeling.

The Black Tenebrionid Beetle is endemic to the Namib and makes good use of condensed fog or dew by 'fog-basking'. Normally active during the day, at night it emerges from its resting place in soft dune-slipface sand to take advantage of nocturnal fog when it occurs. The beetle climbs to the crest of the dune, where fog condensation is greatest, and stands head-down while facing into the fog-bearing wind. Water droplets trickle down its body towards its mouth and are swallowed.

Desert Ants are very social insects, but only where members of their own ant colony are concerned; every other insect is aggressively attacked. Turning to face danger, this species of ant in the Namib Desert curves its abdomen forward under its body in order to spray formic acid, an irritant, at the enemy.

Another species of Tenebrionid Beetle endemic to the Namib has a hard carapace or shell, which acts as a sun shield. The white colouring is from a covering of fine waxy filaments, like a bed of hairs, which slow down water loss in fierce heat by trapping water vapour between them.

The gemsbok is a powerfully built antelope, easily recognizable by its magnificent V-shaped horns and distinctive facial markings. Living in areas where there is always a shortage of water, the gemsbok's resourcefulness in obtaining moisture from melons, succulent roots, and bulbs allows it to survive in one of the hottest places on earth without ever drinking water. It also has a special blood-cooling system in its head, which helps to avoid overheating of its brain.

The ostrich can make a good living in a seemingly desolate habitat like the dry Tsauchab riverbed in the Namib Desert. Adult ostriches eat only plant material that contains 70% water. They therefore do not usually need to drink, although during a severe drought many birds may gather at waterholes in southern Africa's desert regions. The ostrich is the largest living bird on Earth. It is flightless, but can run as fast as 50 km/h.

The Tsauchab River's source is in the Naukluft Mountains of Namibia. Only when there has been a sufficiently long wet season with a large enough volume of water to push westwards beyond the parched plains to the sand of the Namib Desert does the river carry water to the pan called Sossus Vlei. It rarely happens, but when it does the normally cracked dry mud is transformed into an oasis.

Wind in the desert has a profound influence on plants, especially short-lived ones, because of its drying effect in an environment that is already parched. However, wind also widely distributes seeds and other plant materials that are important sources of food for many animal species. Even though the wind may be strong enough to change the shape of a dune's crest, tiny animals like beetles or lizards moving across the surface are not blown away because wind speed decreases the closer it is to the ground.

Above
The Tractrac Chat, which is often seen in the Namib, is named after the *trak-trak* sound it sometimes makes on takeoff. When it lands, it flicks its wings and jerks its tail. Its nest is a neat cup on the ground.

From a distance the Black-backed Jackal looks like a small dog wearing a thick black saddle spangled with silver-white. During winter in the drier western areas its overall colouring, particularly the male's, becomes much redder. It does not need to drink water regularly. Being omnivorous, its food items vary with the nature of the terrain and availability, and include both live prey and carrion. It is one of few mammalian species that have a long-term pair bond, the males assisting in the feeding, guarding and rearing of the pups.

Following spread
The Greater Flamingo is one of two species of flamingo that occur in big flocks on large bodies of shallow water, saline or brackish, inland or coastal, in the desert regions. Hundreds of flamingos congregate at Walvis Bay.

Lichens are the first plants to colonize bare rock or soil. Vast lichen fields cover seemingly empty gravel and gypsum plains of the Namib. These wonder plants exist in extremely harsh conditions but they have no leaves, stems or roots to trap water. Their secret is that they are part fungus and part alga and can absorb water from the air. In the Namib they are dependent on fog for their survival. After receiving even a tiny amount of water, they 'bloom'. Their bright colours make the rock on which a Cape Bunting perches (right) look as though it has been splashed with paint.

Following spread
Bradfield's Namib Day Gecko relies on its colouring to conceal it from both predators and prey. In the early morning it basks in the sun to warm up; during the heat of the day it hangs onto the shaded side of a rock to cool down. It is endemic to a very small area of the Namib Desert between the Kuiseb River and Twyfelfontein in western Damaraland.

The weird and wonderful Welwitschia has been described as a living fossil. Some living Welwitschias are at least 2 000 years old. They are among the rarest plants on Earth, numbering only a few thousand sparsely scattered over the extreme western strip of the Namib Desert from the Kuiseb River in Namibia to southwestern Angola. The plant has only two leaves growing out from opposite sides of its stem, but it looks as if there are more because wind shreds them into many strips. They keep on growing throughout its life and can reach a width of two metres.

The dry river courses in Kaokoland have subterranean water that sustains comparatively rich vegetation. This in turn supports a wide variety of animals, including elephants. These elephants are not a separate species but a type of African Elephant that has adapted to survival in the desert. They move great distances between their feeding grounds and waterholes or springs, and drink only every third or fourth day. In this environment trees are very scarce and Desert Elephants are careful not to debark or uproot them. In the dry season the elephants browse, but during the rains they eat more grass, which gives the trees time to recover.

Hereros are members of a group of Bantu-speaking peoples of the western desert regions of Namibia, Angola and South Africa. Their traditions claim that their origins were in the Great Rift Valley of East Africa, and that they arrived in present-day Namibia in the mid-sixteenth century. They used to be semi-nomadic; today they reside in villages and mainly rear goats. In the early nineteenth century, Herero women adopted the style of dress worn by women who came with missionary settlers to what was then South West Africa. Colourful long dresses and horn-shaped headdresses became their national costume and remain so today.

The Himba people of remote northwestern Namibia are related to the Hereros and their lifestyle indicates how the Hereros probably used to live before they adopted European ways. Himbas have remained nomadic and their characteristic small-scale consumption of the Namib's scarce resources is a living example of ancient human survival strategy in the desert biome. The traditional dress of married Himba women is a bare torso, bare feet, a head adornment and a multilayered goatskin skirt. One of their daily tasks is the fetching of water, and the small size of their containers shows how extremely frugal is their use of it.

Following spread

Himba women use ochre and mud in their hair, clothing and adornments, and a mixture of butter, ash and ochre on their skin as a protection against sunburn and the drying effect of their windy environment. Their iron, leather and ostrich-eggshell jewellery is traditionally passed on from mother to daughter.

SUCCULENT DESERT

The so-called 'Succulent Desert' is better known to botanists and ecologists as the Succulent Karoo. It lies in a winter-rainfall region in the extreme southwestern part of the southern African deserts, stretching from about Lüderitz in the north, southwards along the Atlantic coast to around Lambert's Bay, then eastwards inland into the westernmost parts of the Little Karoo. Its main physical features are shrubby plains of sand or stones and rocky mountains and hills, or 'broken country'. The winter rainfall, mainly in the form of light drizzle, originates as cold fronts from the cool Atlantic Ocean and is more predictable than the rain in other desert regions. Though the winters are chilly, frost seldom occurs.

About 5 000 species of plants occur in the Succulent Desert, of which 4 000 are succulents and just under half are endemic. Most of them belong to two main families, the Mesembryanthemums ('Mesems') and the Crassulas. Grasses and trees are rare or absent.

In the long, dry summers air temperatures are often over 40° C, and the land has a rather bleak aspect, but after the first winter rains the veld undergoes a swift and extraordinary change as carpets of flowers cover the earth, often as far as the eye can see. Fields of orange, purple, pink, white and yellow dazzle the eye. These ephemeral plants survive the dry season in the form of seeds and most belong to the daisy family, though many succulent perennial Mesems also contribute to the colourful display. After rain the seeds germinate quickly, flower in a few days, set seed and die back again, taking full advantage of the short-lived moisture in the soil. These spectacular plants that give Namaqualand its spring colours are a major tourist attraction.

Not all the plants store water in their leaves or stems above ground: many do so in underground organs, such as bulbs, corms or swollen roots that provide a valuable food source to many animals, especially digging and burrowing mammals. These plants are called 'geophytes' and are not strictly regarded as succulents.

Why do succulent plants dominate in the winter-rainfall area of the southern African deserts? The answer is linked not only to the need to survive the long, dry summer months, but also to the fairly predictable rainfall in the Succulent Karoo: these plants can grow during the cold winters when the soil is moist. This contrasts with plants in the summer-rainfall deserts and in those arid regions where rainfall is unpredictable, which thrive at high temperatures.

There are 88 species of vertebrate animals in the Succulent Desert, of which 25 are endemic. Most of these are reptiles, as is the case among the Namib endemic vertebrates. There are two species of snake, a tortoise and sixteen species of lizard. Two of these reptiles are of special interest, namely the Namaqua Dwarf Chameleon and the Namaqua Dwarf Adder. This smallest of adders reaches a maximum recorded length of 28 centimetres and behaves much like the other small desert adders, shuffling its body into loose sand, leaving only its head exposed to keep a lookout for frogs and geckos. The Namaqua Dwarf Chameleon is a patchwork of dull grey, green, cream and brown with a pale yellow streak from behind the head to the front of the body, but when disturbed it loses these colours and becomes plain grey. Courting males become dark blue with a reddish stripe around the scales on the sides of the body. The Namaqua Chameleon, a different species altogether, is not in fact endemic to the succulent desert, but occurs in the Karoo and almost the whole of the Namib.

The Namaqua Day Gecko is also endemic to the Succulent Desert where it is active by day, foraging among the plants for small insects. It is marvellously camouflaged in its pattern of grey with paler speckles and spots, blending in with the granite of its chosen home. Three species of frog are also endemic to the Succulent Desert. No species of bird is endemic to this habitat, but birdlife is surprisingly rich, including elements from the Nama Karoo, the Namib and the Cape Fynbos. Sunbirds are particularly evident during the flowering season as they search restlessly for nectar.

The one tortoise endemic to the Succulent Karoo is the Speckled Padloper. It lives among the granite hills where it feeds on succulent vegetation. It is still common, even though it has a low breeding rate: the female lays only one egg a year.

The Succulent Karoo is fairly well conserved by a number of

reserves: Richtersveld, Namaqua and Tanqua Karoo National Parks and a proposed Namaqua Coast National Park, as well as provincial reserves like the Goegab Nature Reserve, which includes the Hester Malan Wild Flower Garden. Even so, the region has been heavily overused in the past, especially by sheep and other livestock, and has undergone some serious degradation, mainly as erosion of the shallow soil by wind and rain. There are still problems of overgrazing today.

The Succulent Karoo is one of the most accessible of the arid regions of southern Africa. Roads converge on it from Cape Town in the south, Upington in the east and Namibia in the north. Within the area there are good roads, both tarred and gravel, which take one to every kind of habitat. You can visit the sandy plains towards the coast, the rolling stony country further inland and rocky mountains in the most easterly and northerly parts.

The Richtersveld is one of the most popular destinations at the northern edge of the Succulent Desert bordering the Orange River. It is said to be biologically 'the richest desert in the world' with 2 700 species of plants, of which just over one-fifth are endemic. It also has an almost-endemic snake in the form of the Desert Mountain Adder that lives on the mostly bare rocky mountains and is also found northwards into Namibia as far as Aus on the edge of the Namib Desert; there is also a population of this snake further east around Augrabies Falls on the Orange River. Unlike other small adders of the arid zone, this one cannot bury itself in sand because its habitat is rocky.

Rainfall in this area varies on average from about 40 millimetres a year at the coast to about 300 millimetres per year further inland where precipitation results from cooling of the air as it rises to the tops of the mountains. On the plains rain may not even reach the ground, evaporating in the heated air as it falls.

Two of the Richtersveld's most characteristic and conspicuous plants are the tree-like *Aloe pillansii* and the rare *Pachypodium namaquanum* (known in Afrikaans as the *half-mens* because it looks like a human form). *Aloe pillansii* is very closely related to the Kokerboom or Quiver Tree, a widespread

species in the rocky parts of the southern African deserts, including the Succulent Desert.

Not only does the Richtersveld offer amazing rugged scenery, astonishing plant life and some exciting birdwatching, but it is also inhabited by hardy Nama people who have lived there

for thousands of years and retain their ancestral Nama-Khoin language. Today they farm mainly goats that survive on the sparse vegetation and provide their owners with meat and milk. These animals are even hardier than their human companions and will eat many of the succulent plants, including some potentially toxic species of *Euphorbia*. There are trails in the Richtersveld National Park and one may walk them with trained guides to get the greatest benefit of local knowledge.

Previous spread
The landscape of the Succulent Desert is generally flat, but in the northern parts of the Richtersveld, range after range of forbidding rock mountains form a barrier of austere beauty. The mountains are characterized by an extreme climate with almost no rainfall at the foot of the mountains.

When rain falls in the Succulent Desert, the landscape is transformed into a rich carpet of colourful spring flowers.

Following spread
Although arid, the Succulent Desert is home to a remarkable diversity of plants and small animals. The Richtersveld is said to be biologically the richest desert in the world.

A true Succulent Desert endemic, the rare *Pachypodium namaquanum* almost always tilts towards the north and is therefore sometimes called 'the north pole'. These plants are also known in Afrikaans as *halfmens*, meaning half-human, because in silhouette they look almost like people moving forward with bowed heads.

Following spread
The Desert Rose, *Hermannia stricta*, provides a lively splash of colour when it flowers for up to two months even during a prolonged drought. It is a woody shrub with a perennial rootstock, and the flowers are lantern-shaped.

Above

Most Toad Grasshoppers look like toads, but this *Crypsicerus* species looks so stone-like that it isn't noticed unless it moves.

Opposite

Often called 'living stones' because they resemble the stones around them, *Lithops* (top) are members of the *Mesembryanthemum* family. Their camouflage is to avoid being grazed by herbivores, and their shape is to reduce evaporation. Most of each plant is underground, with only two rounded and flattened leaf tips showing above the soil, but the leaves have 'windows' in them to let in the light.

The flower buds of the low-growing, self-pollinating *Avonia* plants (bottom left) lie flat and dormant until the day of blooming, when they stand up until their seeds have been formed and dispersed. Their leaves are so small they are hardly visible, and their succulent branches are covered with white scales to reduce evaporation.

Known as 'little gems', found throughout the Richtersveld, and clumped together in bare rock cracks, *Conophytum* plants (bottom right) are very small succulents. They resemble *Lithops* except that their stems are cylindrical and their tiny flowers more brightly coloured.

Gordon's Hoodia thrives in very hot and dry places where its succulent stems have thorns to protect them from being grazed by herbivores, and spiny angles that help them to reduce evaporation by scattering and reflecting the sun's rays. Its leathery flowers have a putrid smell that attracts pollinating flies. The Khoisan people have used this plant for centuries as an appetite suppressant when food is scarce.

Opposite

A member of the daisy family, *Euryops namibensis* is an unusual shrub found in the Succulent Desert because it is woody. Its branches are covered with small leaves, and its eye-catching flower heads reflect its generic name, *Euryops*, meaning large eye.

Previous spread

The Quiver Tree is a slow-growing tree-succulent of the genus

The perennial succulent *Stapelia gariepensis* is endemic to arid areas of 'broken country' along the lower Orange River

Many species of *Mesembryanthemum* are scattered across rocky hills in Namaqualand and Richtersveld. Perhaps because of insect preference 'Mesems' have evolved to produce many brilliant colours, but none of them is blue. Shiny flowers are a feature of all the succulent plants in this family and the purpose appears to be to attract insects for pollination. No insects eat the petals, but all those that visit relish the pollen.

Previous spread

The geological history of the immensely old rocks and sediments in the magnificence of the Richtersveld is the subject of ongoing research.

Opposite

When desert plants bloom in response to rain, an abundance of insects, rodents, and other small creatures also occurs. This in turn attracts bird species such as the highly nomadic Black-shouldered Kite (left) that would otherwise not be found in desert places.

Above

Rain falls in winter but infrequently in the Succulent Desert, so seeds lie dormant in the soil until conditions become favourable for them to germinate and grow. Then, within a few days, flowers like orange *Gazania* and purple *Felicia* bloom for a short time, set seed and die back again. In an intensely competitive environment, it's all about versatility in finding survival options for the sake of future generations of plants. The tall yellow *Bulbinella* stores food and moisture in an underground bulb and is therefore less dependent on rainfall for its flowering.

The Nama people in Namaqualand and the Richtersveld are descendants of a branch of the Khoi-Khoi. Their language resembles that of the Bushmen in having mainly monosyllabic roots and explosive consonants that produce 'click' sounds. They are traditionally pastoral, and raise sheep, goats, cattle and horses.

Below
Research has shown that rocks in this area of the Richtersveld were deposited by melting glaciers during one of the earliest-known ice ages. There is also evidence of early hunter-gatherer, and later herder, presence near this present-day settlement called Kuboes. There are few clusters of permanent dwellings in this thirstland because herding families tend to be nomadic, having constantly to move their flocks according to seasonal availability of water and food.

Homeward bound with firewood for cooking and aromatic herbs to freshen her home, this Nama woman is wearing the same kind of cloth sunbonnet or kappie that early Afrikaner women used to wear. Nama culture is rich in music and folk tales, proverbs and poetry that have been handed down traditionally for millennia. Most of the spectacular flowering plants in the Succulent Desert, like these Cape Daisies, *Arctotis fastuosa*, are 'pioneers'. They are the first to take hold on bare ground after disturbance such as grazing or ploughing, and bloom shortly after rain. The Cape Daisy's glossy flowers open fully only in sunshine, and close in cloudy weather and at night to protect the fertile portion of the plant for use in pollination. Their abundant, lightweight seeds are dispersed by wind.

Nama Karoo

The Nama Karoo (or simply 'the Karoo') is a summer-rainfall region of over 600 000 square kilometres. It hugs the Succulent Karoo and the Namib Desert along its western boundary where the annual rainfall averages about 140 millimetres a year. Along its eastern edge it merges with the arid savanna and the sandy vistas of the Kalahari. Rainfall increases from west to east, reaching a maximum annual average of about 500 millimetres, but is unpredictable and droughts occur 30-50% of the time. The region covers much of South Africa from the southwestern Free State and eastern Cape to most of the northern Cape, most of southern Namibia and a narrow strip ending in southern Angola.

Karoo vegetation consists mostly of low woody shrubs and some grass. The more easterly parts of the Karoo are grassier than those further west. The land is mostly rather flat with typically flat-topped hills and a few fairly low mountain ranges. Trees, often thorny, are confined mostly to the dry watercourses, except for hardy species such as the widespread Kokerboom or Quiver Tree. Summer temperatures reach well over 40° C by day and winter nights often drop to –15° C, when frost is common.

In order to survive the harsh climate, Karoo plants have adapted in various ways. The stem may be barrel-shaped, or the whole plant rounded to reduce the surface area and therefore loss of water by evaporation. Leaves may be reduced or lost, to be replaced by green stems for photosynthesis. Euphorbias show these features particularly well. Some species of Acacia fold their compound leaves by day and turn the blades vertically to reduce the surface area exposed to the sun.

The Karoo is reputed to have more than 7 000 species of plants, many of which are endemic to the region. Over 100 species of vertebrates live here, of which 18 or 19 are endemic: nine or ten reptiles, five mammals and four birds – Cinnamonbreasted Warbler, Karoo Lark, Sclater's Lark and Black-eared Sparrowlark. Like most Old World deserts, the Karoo has many other species of larks whose distribution extends into neighbouring habitats. Other ground-dwelling birds include coursers and korhaans.

The two tortoises endemic to the Karoo are the Greater and Karoo Padlopers ('road walkers'), both small species measuring only about 10-13 centimetres in length. The Karoo Padloper is strictly confined to this region, whereas the Greater Padloper is also found in the mountains of southeastern Lesotho. The commonest snake in the Karoo is the Karoo Sand Snake, a species that hunts lizards even in the heat of the day; its range extends into Namibia and the Free State. The only snakes endemic to the Karoo are Fisk's House Snake, the Plain Mountain Adder and the Namib Tiger Snake, but some species, such as the Cape Cobra and the Horned Adder have the Karoo as a centre of distribution. The remaining endemic reptiles are lizards, namely three species of girdled lizards, a dwarf chameleon and a gecko.

The most conspicuous wild mammal in the Karoo is the springbok, which used to occur in tens of thousands, but is today reduced to small herds here and there on farms. It has been unable to compete successfully with domestic stock for grazing, especially sheep, and fencing has hampered its ancient nomadic movements. Under natural conditions the Karoo supported such huge herds because they used the grazing selectively and moved on when it was scarce.

The Karoo has been strongly affected for the worse by poor stock-farming practices. Domestic animals damage the veld, especially during droughts, because brittle plants that would otherwise recover during the next rains are constantly trampled by the resident stock. The carrying capacity of the Karoo varies from one to two sheep per hectare, depending on the quality of grazing. Higher stocking rates than this lead to deterioration of the veld and even to local extinction of some plant species. This in turn leads to sheet and donga erosion and loss of precious soil. As stated by David Shearing in his book *South African wild flower guide 6: Karoo*: '… the flora of this area is of prime importance to those that farm here and must be conserved at all costs as it cannot be replaced by anything else.' He reinforces this by stating that there is not enough water to irrigate artificial pastures. Fortunately the seeds of Karoo plants may remain dormant in the seedbed for up to 70 years and still germinate, so the veld has a chance to recover if given enough protection and time.

Most of the mammals endemic to the Karoo are small rodents. The others are an Elephant Shrew and the endangered Riverine Rabbit. Several species of rodents have their centres of distribution in the Karoo, though they may extend into the Namib, the Succulent Desert and the Arid Savanna. The same may be said of three small carnivores, the Small Spotted (or Blackfooted) Cat, the suricate and the Yellow Mongoose. The only really large mammal endemic to the Karoo is the Mountain Zebra, which occurs in two populations – one in the Cape Mountains and one in the mountains of the Namibian escarpment.

Interestingly, several of the small desert mammals are diurnal, though usually active only in the cooler parts of the day: the Round-eared Elephant Shrew, the Dassie Rat, two species of Whistling Rat and the Bush Karoo Rat. One tiny mammal is endemic to a single mountain in Namibia, the Brukkaros Pygmy Rock Mouse, which lives on the long-extinct crater rising out of the stony plains north of Keetmanshoop.

The Karoo is famous for its rich fossil beds, especially of dinosaurs and mammal-like reptiles. These date from the time when the area was an inland lake, between 250 million and 190 million years ago. The uniqueness of the Karoo fossil beds is that they show an almost unbroken record of 50 million years. The Karoo National Park has some fascinating displays of these fossils.

Little of the Nama Karoo is under strict conservation protection. The main such area is the Karoo National Park near Beaufort West. Smaller conservation areas include the Karoo Nature Reserve at Graaff-Reinet, the Mountain Zebra National Park near Cradock, Bosberg Nature Reserve at Somerset East and the Augrabies Falls National Park on the Lower Orange River.

Augrabies is one of the scenic wonders of the dry west and should not be missed by visitors to the region. In addition to the spectacular waterfalls and granite gorge, one's eye is immediately caught by the Cape Flat Lizards basking in the warm African sun or scurrying about the rocks. The brightly coloured males are blue, red and yellow, the females

dark brown with three broad cream stripes down the back. On either side of the gorge stretches typical northern Karoo vegetation dominated by species of *Euphorbia*. Another interesting plant is known as *wolftoon* (wolf-toe) in Afrikaans or Namaqua Porkbush in English: its succulent stems put out

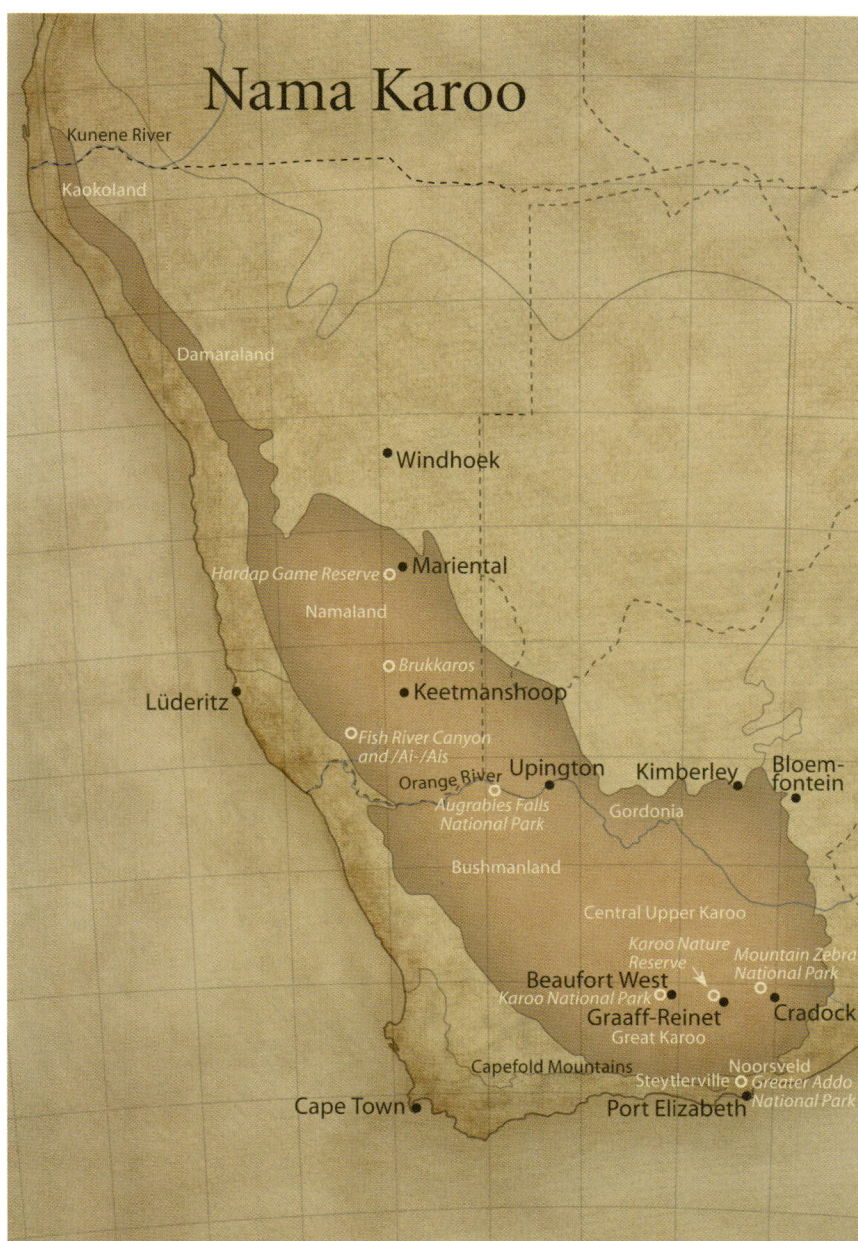

tiny green leaves only under favourable conditions, making it one of the most drought-resistant of the large Karoo plants. A highly characteristic mammal to be seen in this habitat is the charming klipspringer, a small antelope with blunt tips to its hooves, which prevent its slipping on the rocky surfaces.

Above

The Eastern Cape Crag Lizard is a common resident of craggy outcrops on the summits of the Zuurberg Mountains.

Pillars of rock in the Valley of Desolation near Graaff-Reinet overlook a flat landscape with gently undulating hills typical of the Great Karoo.

Whereas flowering Coral Aloes attract many insects, and these in turn attract all kinds of insect-feeding birds such as the bokmakierie, a member of the bush-shrike family, the similar bright colours of Common Milkweed Locusts warn would-be predators that they are distasteful.

The Nama Karoo offers a variety of habitats, such as mountains, plains and wooded areas, ideal for several species of antelope.

Mountain Reedbuck

Klipspringer

Kudu

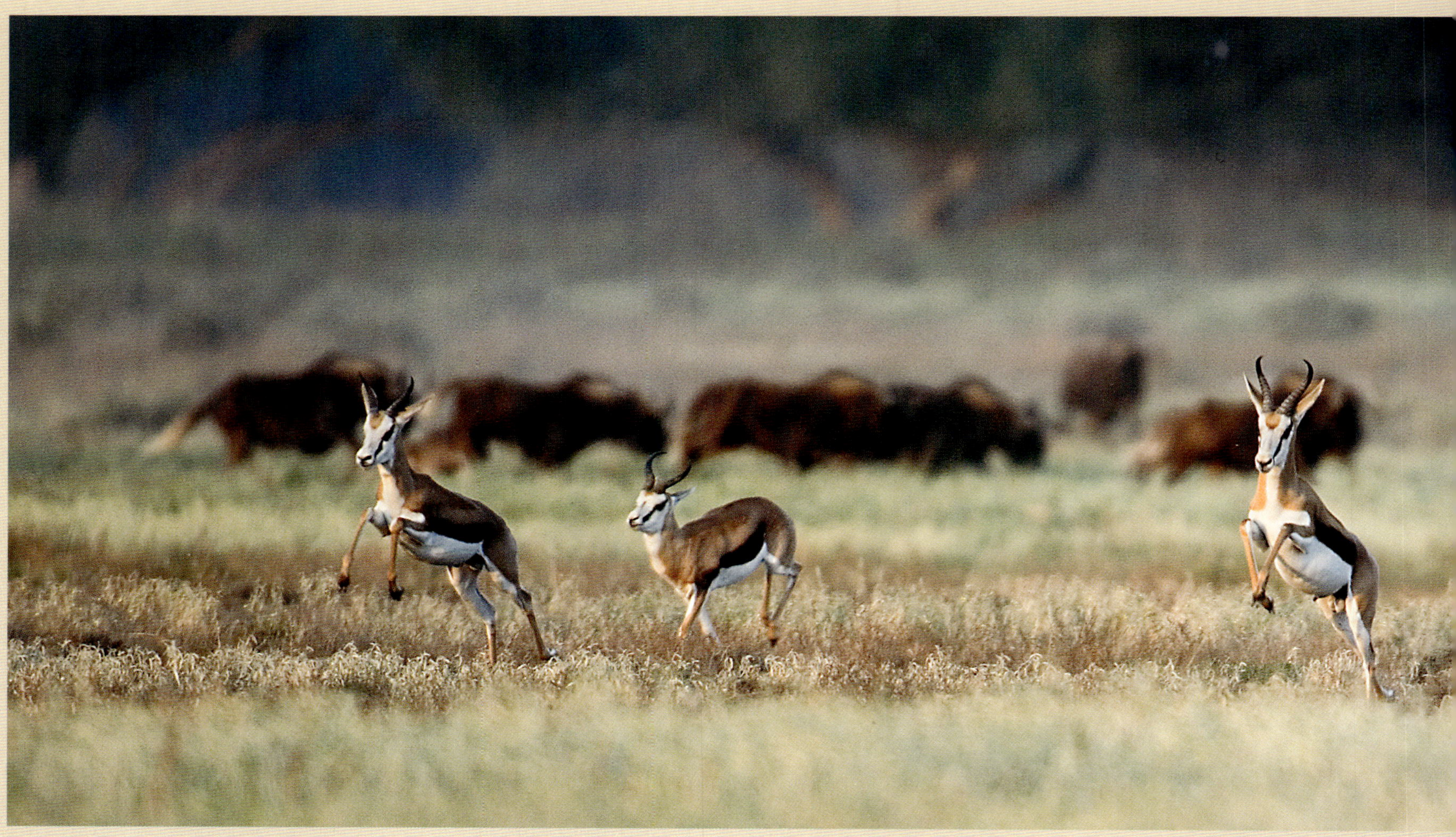

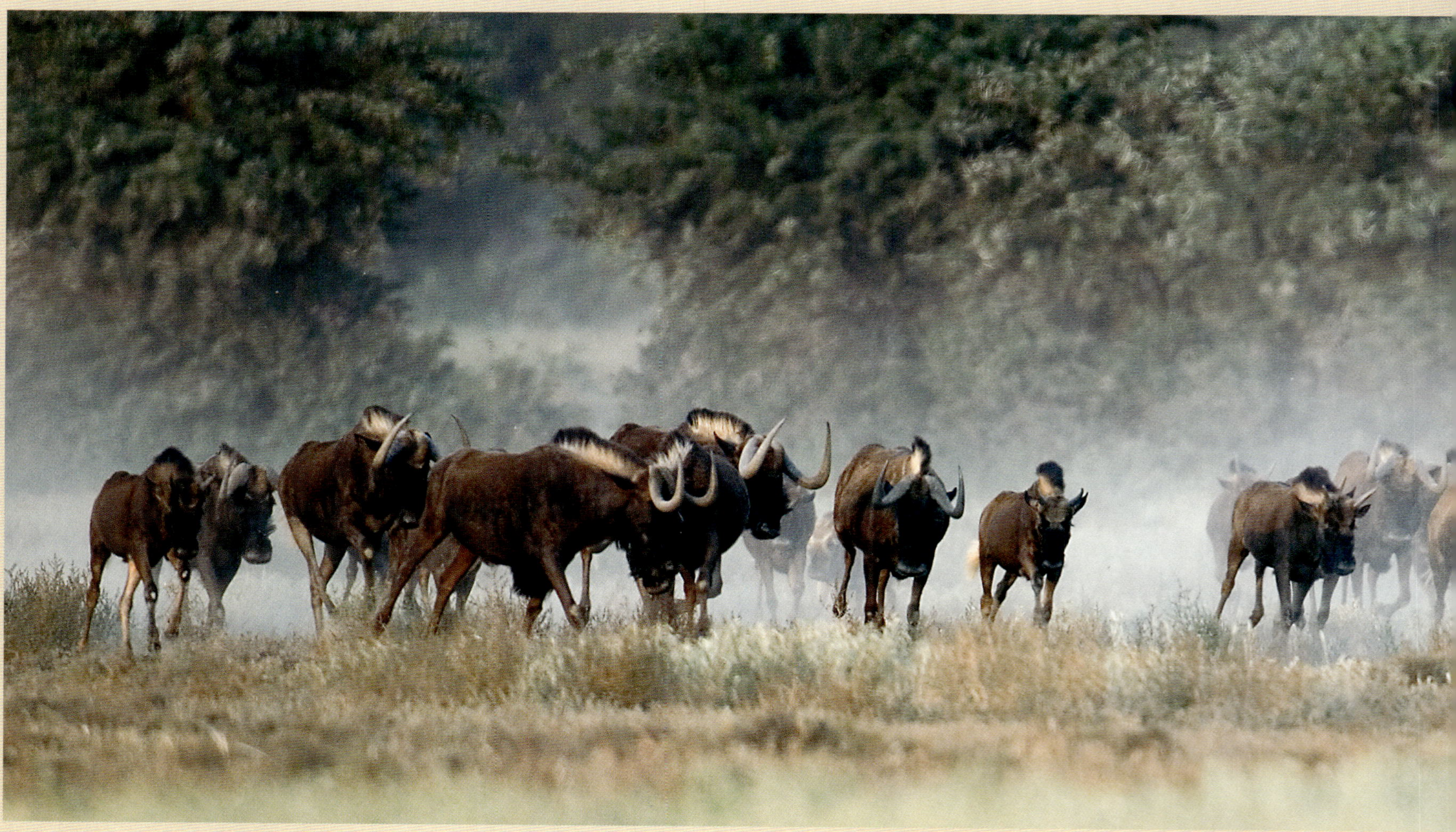

Springbok

Black Wildebeest. Following spread: Blesbok

The Rock Dassie is a species of hyrax that looks like a guinea pig, a rat and a rabbit but is related to the elephants. Each of its toes has a nail and a rubbery pad that help it to climb about the rocky places where it lives. Its blunt muzzle and compact build are adapted for taking shelter and raising its young in crevices. It is exceedingly wary and utters a high-pitched *whit-she* call when alarmed, audible from a great distance.

Opposite

The Black-backed Jackal's dentition is designed to handle all types of food, including long canines for catching and holding onto prey, and cheek teeth for crushing, slicing and chewing. A characteristic sound of the African night is the Black-backed Jackal's call, a high, drawn-out howl followed by yaps, especially in winter, its breeding season.

Opposite

The Cape Hare belongs to a widely distributed family of mammals that includes the rabbits, but in southern Africa there is only one rabbit species, the endangered Riverine Rabbit. Hares are mainly nocturnal, feeding on grass and bark. The young grow quickly and are weaned and independent by about one month old.

Above

Karoo Korhaans lay one or two eggs on bare ground among small shrubs and stones on the open plains of the arid Karoo. They are endemic to western South Africa and southern Namibia, and because they favour disturbed ground, their numbers have actually increased owing to livestock-grazing practices.

Quiver Trees are a familiar sight in the northern parts of the Nama Karoo. The Quiver Tree Forest near Keetmanshoop in southern Namibia is one of the best places to see them in large numbers.

The caracal is an important predator in the Karoo ecosystem.
Although it is sometimes called a Red Lynx, the caracal is
not a true lynx like that of the northern hemisphere. The
Afrikaans name rooikat (red cat) is descriptive of its reddish
colour and catlike behaviour. Its strong back legs are higher
than its shoulders and help it to sprint after its prey, or leap
up in the air to catch a bird in flight. An unusual feature of
the caracal is its black-tufted ears, which are also black at
the back.

Following spreads
The Orange River, whose source is in the highlands of
Lesotho, cuts across the Nama Karoo biome and is one of
only two perennial rivers in the desert regions of southern
Africa. In full flood the thundering Augrabies Falls on the
lower Orange can be heard 40 kilometres away. Their name
is derived from the Nama word, !oukurubes, 'the place
of loud noise'. Amid the silence of a remote and sparsely
populated desert region, these falls drop 148 metres in a
series of preliminary cascades, ending in a final plunge of 60
metres. Equally impressive are the vast areas of surrounding
granitic rock worn slippery smooth by the flow of the river
over millions of years.

After good rains the barren landscape of the Augrabies Falls
National Park is transformed into a green paradise.

Opposite and right
One of the rarest mammals on Earth, the Cape Mountain Zebra is the smallest of the zebras and stands only about a metre high at the shoulder. It looks a lot like Burchell's Zebra, but has a brown muzzle and its stripes don't have 'shadows' between them. It used to occur throughout the mountainous areas of the Nama Karoo but is now mainly found in the Mountain Zebra National Park and Karoo National Park.

Above
The Hartmann's Mountain Zebra is found in dry country where mountains and sand flats meet. It is constantly on the move to where local rain has improved the grazing, covering up to 100 kilometres at a time. It may go deep into the desert if it can find water by digging for it in dry riverbeds. The background colour of its coat is creamy, but often looks brown after the zebra has been dust bathing. In cold weather it stands broadside to the sun to absorb maximum heat. In hot weather it turns its hindquarters, which have a smaller surface area, towards the sun. Its mane is longer than that of the Cape Mountain Zebra.

Karoo rocks contain much of the ancient history of the Earth. Fossils in the rocks reveal an almost unbroken record of 50 million years, with evidence of a rich diversity of dinosaurs and mammal-like reptiles that once lived here. Millions of years ago much of the Karoo was swampland.

Below

In the Sneeuberg range clear impressions of the footprints of dicynodonts were found preserved in a fossilized muddy substrate. Dicynodonts were mammal-like reptiles about the size of a large pig.

Fossilized dicynodont skeleton on display in the Karoo National Park

Fossilized dicynodont footprint at Sante Sana

The Khoisan people named this region *Karoo*, or *!gar-b*, 'dry place' or 'desert', yet this drought-stricken land, without natural surface water, now supports one of the world's largest sheep populations. Thanks to the nineteenth-century invention and production of the wind-pump, great flocks of sheep can survive here by eating scant but nutritious shrubs and satisfying their thirst. According to radiocarbon dating of excavated sheep remains, and some rock paintings of sheep, fat-tailed sheep were already in the Karoo about 1 500 years ago.

Male ostriches show off their feathers in spectacular courtship displays, and in the ostrich-feather industry the finest feathers come from the male birds, which are clipped every year. Since ostriches can live for up to 40 years, a single male can provide a large number of feathers in its lifetime. The great ostrich-feather boom in the Little Karoo began in the late nineteenth century, and lasted more than twenty years while fashionable ladies throughout the world wore feathered hats, capes, gowns, fans and boas. The men who made their fortune in feathers were known as 'feather barons'. The grand homes they built were sumptuous enough to be called 'ostrich palaces'. Ostrich farming continues to be very much a part of the Little Karoo for the supply of other products such as meat, leather and dusters.

Arid Savanna

As the rainfall increases eastwards from the Nama Karoo Desert, so the vegetation becomes denser until trees begin to shape the landscape and grass is a significant ground cover. The result is a savanna. The soil becomes increasingly sandy, especially in the Kalahari (or Kgalagadi) basin that covers much of Botswana and parts of the Northern Cape and Namibia – the Sandveld. Kalahari sand has a high iron content and weathers to a bright orange-red, giving the region a characteristic background colour that is matched by many of its ground-dwelling animals.

Typical trees in this region are Camelthorns, Shepherd's Trees and, in the more northerly parts, Mopane. Camelthorns are mostly confined to the dry riverbeds in the south, but are more widespread in the rather wetter north. The Arid Savanna Desert shares many features with the southern African Bushveld. The presence of trees means that more arboreal birds, mammals and reptiles are found here.

Partly because of its sandy nature, the arid savanna lacks surface water, so its resident animals are independent of drinking water, obtaining from their food all the moisture they require. However, the drilling of boreholes for water has enabled the region to be opened up for stock farming and has allowed previously migratory or nomadic mammals, such as the Blue Wildebeest and springbok, to become resident. This has affected the vegetation to the extent that in many areas, especially where sheep and goats are kept, the plant cover has been removed completely and the sand now drifts with the wind, whereas formerly the plants prevented this. The vegetated dunes are largely fixed in long lines parallel to the prevailing wind direction at the time of their formation.

There are few endemic animals in the arid savanna. Most of the fauna is shared by neighbouring habitats, especially the bushveld further east and north. The only true Kalahari endemic is Woosnam's Desert Rat, a mainly terrestrial species that nevertheless climbs trees in search of food. Though not endemic, the Bushveld Elephant Shrew is one of the few small mammals whose distribution is centred in the Kalahari basin. It is common in the dry central parts of Botswana where the rainfall is less than 450 millimetres a year, and can thrive where it is as low as 200 millimetres a year. Its diet of insects makes it independent of other water sources.

Another small mammal common in the Kalahari, but not confined to it, is the Tree Mouse, which feeds on green leaves and seed pods, allowing it too to be free of the need to drink water. Its large stick nests are a conspicuous feature in Camelthorn trees in the Nossob River in the Kgalagadi Transfrontier Park. One of the few species of bat to be found in such dry places is Dent's Horseshoe Bat which lives in caves in the Tsodilo Hills and in Drotsky's Caves in Botswana.

The sandy soil allows many kinds of mammals to burrow – rodents (including Ground Squirrels), mongooses, honey badgers, hyenas, pangolins, aardwolves and others. Living in an underground burrow, combined in some cases with nocturnal activity, allows these animals to escape the stress of daytime heat. But it also means that they have to share their homes with snakes and often with others of their own species.

Three very common snakes in the Arid Savanna Desert are the Cape Cobra, the puff adder and the molesnake. They are all avid rodent-eaters, so they have a good food supply at their disposal. The Cape Cobra is also an adept tree climber; it preys on Tree Mice and raids the nests of the Sociable Weaver, one of the arid savanna's most characteristic birds. As you drive through the Northern Cape and Namibia you will see the huge communal nests of this amazing sparrow-sized bird. Each nest mass looks like a thatched roof and has several dozen nest chambers, each of which is reached by a short vertical tunnel from below and occupied in the breeding season by a pair of Sociable Weavers and their chicks.

Other species of birds also use the nest masses of Sociable Weavers as breeding or roosting places. The most famous 'guest' is the Pygmy Falcon, a bird of prey hardly bigger than a shrike. A pair of falcons usually takes over one or two chambers in the nest mass – one for breeding and one for roosting. Although the guests sometimes eat their hosts, they don't do so often enough to cause the arrangement to break down.

Red sand is the favoured habitat of several species of larks and reptiles, whose coloration matches that of the sand to perfection. Perhaps the commonest sand-dwelling snake of the region is the Horned Adder, different populations of which are coloured to match their backgrounds, whether they inhabit the Namib, the Karoo or the sandveld. There are at least three species of snake endemic to the Arid Savanna, and one tortoise, the Kalahari Tent Tortoise. Of the many species of lizards, which include skinks, agamas and geckos, only four are endemic. One subspecies of the Common Barking Gecko is also endemic to the Kalahari: its *chuck-chuck-chuck* 'barking' is a feature of warm nights. By day it lives in a shallow burrow, often in wind-blown sand against a shrub.

Birdlife in the Arid Savanna is rich and varied, but only Burchell's Sandgrouse is endemic to the red sands. Its rich salmon colouring renders it perfectly suited to its background. Like all sandgrouse, it feeds on dry seeds and has to drink almost every day, so it is absent from large parts of the south-western Kalahari sandveld. The same applies to the seed-eating Black-cheeked Waxbill. The Violet-eared Waxbill, whose centre of distribution is also in the Kalahari, rivals this pretty little bird in its bright colours.

At least 14 other species of birds are centred in the Kalahari, but not confined to it. Such terrestrial species as the Fawn-coloured Lark, as well as the other dune-living larks, are typically rich pinkish to rusty red as an adaptation to their background. There are patches in the Kalahari where prevailing winds have blown the sand away to reveal the underlying pale grey limestone flats, and the birds that live there are coloured grey, or have patterned plumage to camouflage them on the stony ground.

Along the banks of some of the bigger dry rivers, such as the Auob and the Nossob, the limestone forms low cliffs, in some of which are caves or overhangs where leopards find shelter for bearing their cubs. The large number of grazing ungulates in the Arid Savanna supports large predators like leopards, lions and cheetahs, at least where they are protected in game reserves such as the Kgalagadi Transfrontier Park, the Central Kalahari Game Reserve and Etosha National Park. These reserves are a paradise for tourists, not only for seeing the big-

game mammals, but for observing their exciting birdlife too.

Most of the Arid Savanna in Namibia and the Northern Cape of South Africa is given over to stock farming, but large tracts of Botswana are still pristine. These places are the last stronghold of the Bushmen or San people, most of whom were

exterminated in the rest of southern Africa. These remarkable people, of whom nearly 60 000 exist today, live mainly in Botswana and Namibia. Those who are still hunter-gatherers exhibit an astonishing ability to survive under the harshest environmental conditions. Now that they are no longer persecuted by later arrivals to southern Africa – the Bantu-speaking people and the white settlers – they should continue to exist as an integral part of this diverse subcontinent.

Camelthorn Trees are popular nesting sites for gregarious White-browed Sparrow-Weavers (previous spread) and other common desert birds such as Sociable Weavers (below). Nests with eggs and chicks attract predators such as the Cape Cobra (below), against which the adults have no defence. The snake can consume the entire contents of a Sociable Weaver colony in one visit.

Camelthorn Trees also provide shelter for various other animals such as the African Wild Cat that closely resembles the domestic cat but is recognizable by the red colour at the back of its ears, and its long, slender legs. Because it readily interbreeds with domestic cats, many hybrids occur in the smaller protected areas, and the distinguishing features of the wild cat are progressively lost in the offspring.

Previous spread
Although the leopard is the most widespread predator in desert areas, and still occurs outside conservation areas on farms and close to settlements, it is generally nocturnal and therefore seldom seen. It will take any kind of prey, from small rodents to large antelopes. Using any cover available, it stalks its prey until it is close enough to pounce on it and deliver the killing bite.

The South African Crested Porcupine is the largest rodent in southern Africa. In the absence of a complete covering of hair, it has a high fat content to keep its body warm. This makes it irresistible to predators like leopards and lions, even though they risk severe infection and possible death from contact with the porcupine's razor-sharp quills.

In the past, lions occurred widely in desert areas, even on the Skeleton Coast, wherever prey was available to them. With increasingly dense settlement by humans in their ancestral territory, the distribution of lions has shrunk to the extent that they now occur only in some private game reserves and in large conservation areas such as Etosha, Central Kalahari, and Kgalagadi Transfrontier Park.

Depending on the size of its home range, a lion pride usually consists of from one to four adult males, several adult females (one of them dominant), and young of various ages. The number of cubs in a lioness's litter is regulated by the availability of food.

Blue Wildebeest are mostly seen in large herds moving in single file, bound for water and pasture. In arid terrain they often have to cover great distances to find water to drink, and can survive for up to five days without it. Blue Wildebeest are always favourite prey for lions. After a kill, a cub may carry a bone as a plaything.

Following spreads
Although lions often kill gemsbok, these antelopes know when lions are not hunting. They keep a watchful eye and a respectful distance and will dash away if they sense danger.

Sometimes a lion will kill other predators or their young, such as Bat-eared Foxes or cheetah cubs, but not eat them. Since this type of predation is not for food, it is possibly a lion's instinctive way to reduce competition for food resources.

Although the honey badger is so named because it likes bee larvae and honey, rodents like Brant's Whistling Rat are a regular part of its diet. The badger digs the rat out of the ground with its long claws, and then carries it away to feed.

The Brown Hyena (above), like the aardwolf (left), occupies an old antbear hole as a shelter. The main difference between them lies in their feeding habits; the aardwolf is an insect specialist and feeds mainly on termites, while the Brown Hyena is more of a generalist. Its diet consists mainly of carrion, supplemented with insects, rodents, birds, fruit and eggs.

Opposite

Formerly much hunted for its beautiful coat, the only true fox found in Africa, the Cape Fox, is now considered rare. It is quite small, weighing only two to three kilograms, even with its thick fur coat, and stands only 30 centimetres high at the shoulder. Active mainly at dawn and dusk, it feeds mostly on mice and insects. During the day it rests up in a burrow that it digs for itself, or in a thicket, and so it is seldom seen.

At close quarters in its natural habitat, the magnificent cheetah is as breathtaking as when seen in its high-speed, jinking pursuit of prey. Its name is derived from the Hindi *chita*, meaning 'spotted'. It is the fastest land mammal on Earth, but can maintain its maximum speed only in the final 100 to 300 metres of the chase, after which it is too tired to continue. If successful in bringing down its prey, it needs about half an hour to catch its breath before it can begin to eat its meal.

Wildlife reserves like Namibia's Etosha National Park afford visitors an opportunity to experience a natural congregation of animals at a waterhole, that in zoos are kept apart. The giraffe, about five metres tall, is the tallest animal in the world. The eland is the largest of the African antelopes, adult males standing about 1.6 metres high at the shoulder and weighing up to 700 kilograms. 'There can be no such animal', it was declared of the Burchell's Zebra, named after the nineteenth-century explorer, William Burchell, who took the original specimen from South Africa and presented it to the British Museum.

Following spread

An elephant's nose is used for much more than just smelling and breathing. It forms a long, powerful trunk that acts as an arm and a hand in eating, drinking, caressing, trumpeting, seizing, weight bearing, tree felling and fighting. The size of an African Elephant's tusks is an indication of its diet. Elephants that live in a desert biome such as those found in Namibia's Etosha National Park, Damaraland and Kaokoland, have shorter tusks than bushveld-dwelling elephants in the wetter Kruger National Park of South Africa. These Desert Elephants' tusks are brown because they frequently have to dig underground for water.

Cape Sparrows (above) and Cape Turtle-doves (left) congregate in large numbers to drink in the early morning, a time of day when various predators, including birds of prey such as the immature Lanner Falcon (right), are lurking nearby. If a predator dashes in for the kill, it is confused by the 'blur effect' of many of them taking off together.

Burchell's Sandgrouse is endemic to the red sand of the Kalahari Desert, where it nests in a shallow scrape under a grass tuft or shrub. It feeds exclusively on dry seeds throughout its life and needs to drink daily. Two to four hours after sunrise, it flies up to 80 kilometres to a waterhole. It drinks very quickly, and then takes off straight out of the water, rapidly calling *wok-wok-wok* as it flies away. However, if it is a breeding male sandgrouse whose chicks are too young to fly long distances, its behaviour is quite different. First it rubs its belly in dry sand to remove waterproofing on the feathers. Then it walks into the water and, keeping its wings dry, bobs up and down to soak up water in its belly feathers. When it flies back to its chicks they drink the water from its feathers. Adult females have an ochre-coloured throat; adult males have a grey throat.

If disturbed, many ground-nesting birds like the Kori Bustard attempt to protect their vulnerable eggs or young with a 'distraction display'. This female has increased her size by inflating her neck feathers, raising her tail, fanning it out to display its eye-catching black-and-white bands, and drooping her wings to reveal the striking mottled pattern on their edges. Weighing up to 19 kilograms, the Kori Bustard is the heaviest flying bird in the world.

Opposite page

Most birds use characteristic calls and visual displays to convey information about their gender, territory, readiness to breed and pair formation, and also to maintain their pair bond. During his courtship display the Northern Black Korhaan male stands on some elevation calling loudly, *kraak kraaak*, and then flies up. He cruises around his territory, calling, before descending slowly with flapping wings and dangling yellow legs.

Jet-black and crimson, the Crimson-breasted Shrike is all the more striking when seen against the back-drop of the barren-looking habitat in which this bird is found. In the Arid Savanna it lives in Acacia thickets, dry river courses, and scrub. The bill is hooked at the tip for dealing with hard-bodied insect prey. This type of predatory bill is common to all bush-shrikes, which is why the bird is called a shrike, but, unlike the true shrikes, it does not impale its prey on thorns.

The Swallow-tailed Bee-eater has a deeply forked tail like a swallow's that helps it to manoeuvre in flight and catch its food in the air. The bird's long bill helps it to keep a stinging insect a safe distance from its head. It brings the insect to a perch, and rubs it against the perch to remove its sting before swallowing it. The bird also uses its long bill to dig a nesting burrow in a sandbank.

Above

A suricate has strong, curved claws on its front feet that enable it to dig for food in soft sand as well as stony ground.

Opposite

In summer after rain when the sand is firm, a female Ground Agama digs a shallow hole in sandy soil in which to lay her eggs.

Whirlwinds often precede rain, which comes in the form of short, violent thunderstorms. Rain brings new life to the desert.

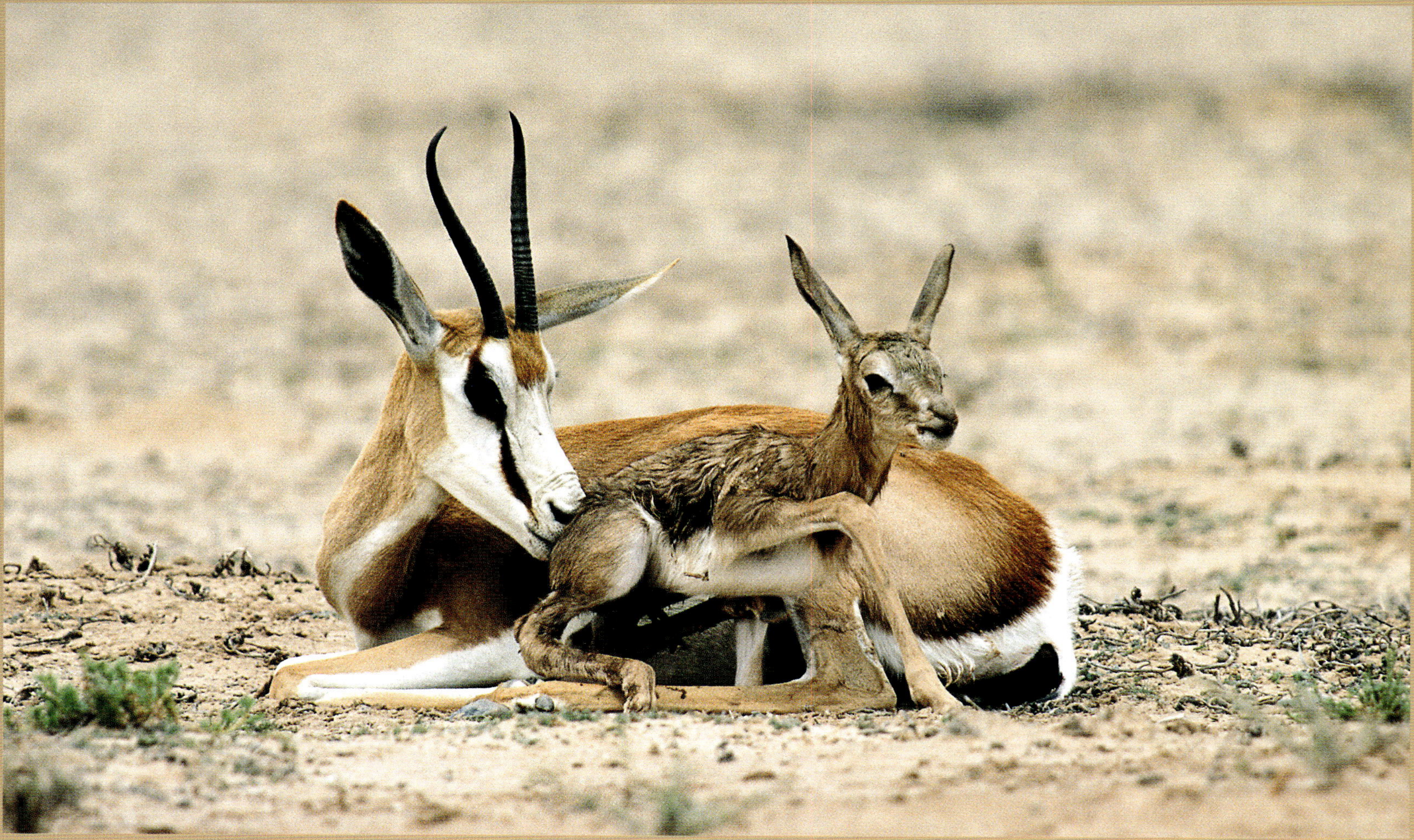

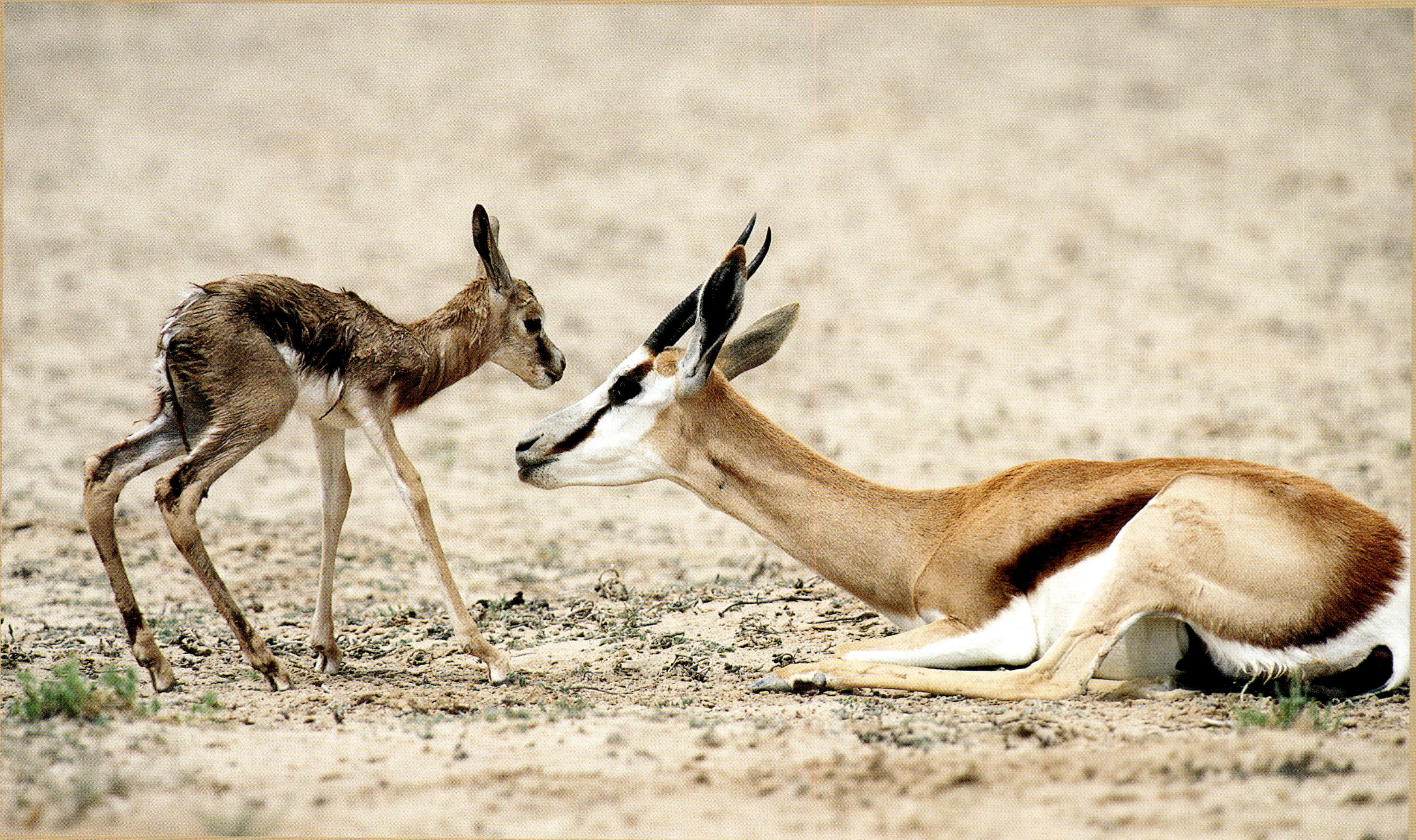

Good rains stimulate springbok to drop their lambs. When a female springbok feels her time for giving birth approaching, she separates herself from the rest of the herd. Mother and newborn lamb are continuously vulnerable to predation, so it is essential for their survival that the lamb is mobile within minutes of birth. The mother nudges her lamb's rump to encourage it to stand, and then there is a mutual imprinting of smell. Eventually the lamb manages to keep upright by splaying its legs. Once it can lift a foot without falling over in a heap, its mother guides it to her teats so that it can begin suckling.

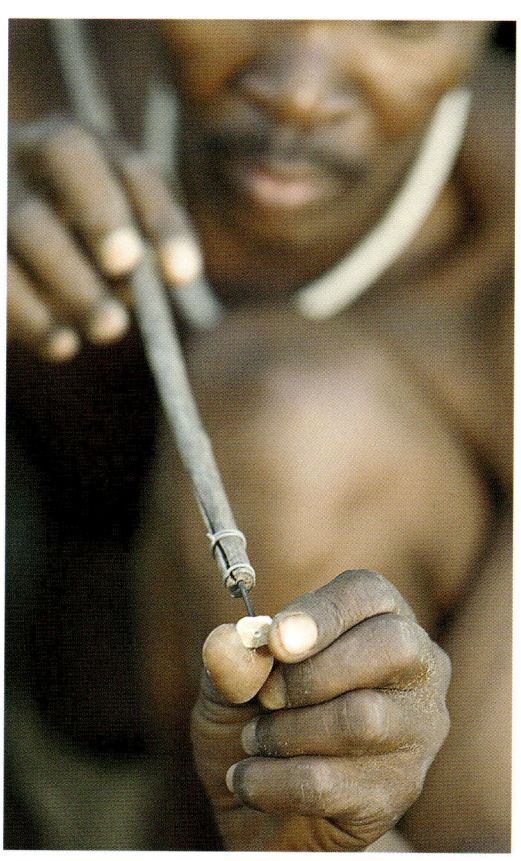

The San people descended from the original hunting and gathering groups who occupied southern Africa 150 000 years ago. They are a living archive of historically valuable records of our transition from the Old Stone Age developmental period of humans who were hunters, through the Neolithic Stone Age when people took the first steps in agriculture, the domestication of animals, weaving and pottery, to our present way of life.

FUTURE WISE

What does the future hold for the long-term conservation of the desert environment? Are present and proposed measures adequate? One of the most useful concepts that has arisen in recent years is that of 'Transfrontier Parks' or 'Peace Parks', generally termed Transfrontier Conservation Areas or TFCAs. They transcend political boundaries, increase the size of conservation areas and allow greater freedom of movement for terrestrial animals that need to migrate or undertake nomadic movements in order to find new feeding grounds. Such mergers have been (or are about to be) implemented between South Africa and neighbouring Namibia, Botswana, Moçambique and Zimbabwe. Angola is also likely to enter the picture in due course.

They are relevant to the arid and semi-arid regions which will see the merging of the Richtersveld National Park in South Africa's Succulent Desert with the /Ai-/Ais region of what is presently the Fish River National Park of Namibia, and eventually the Skeleton Coast Park of Namibia with the Iona National Park of Angola. The Kgalagadi Transfrontier Park already exists; it was formed on 12 May 2000 by the merging of the Kalahari Gemsbok National Park of South Africa and the Gemsbok National Park of Botswana. The Richtersveld is also a 'contractual park' in that the South African National Parks, SANParks, has contracted with its human inhabitants, the Nama or Khoi-Khoin people, to introduce a joint management policy: the Nama inhabit the park and manage it for their own pastoral purposes, as well as for conservation under the guidance of SANParks.

While these steps are to be commended in pure conservation terms, they pose potential problems for the management of these large areas. The first problem is financial: how do such parks meet their running costs? It is generally acknowledged that conservation, which includes tourism and trophy hunting, must be self-sustaining. Tourism is one of the main sources of income, but a fundamental problem in the dry west is the provision of water for tourist facilities. Rainfall is inadequate, so dams are out of the question. Boreholes at present supply all the water for the desert reserves, but their water is

often not suitable for human consumption. Apart from that, depletion of ground water presents a potential long-term environmental problem. Water is therefore a limiting resource.

When the desert parks were first opened to tourism, all visitors had to camp and to carry their own water, food, firewood and other supplies. Roads were poor and facilities non-existent, yet the deserts beckoned and the stream of visitors increased. With increasing popularity and demand for greater convenience, hutted accommodation was established, with running water from boreholes. Tourists demanded ever better facilities until the chalets were upgraded to five-star status, and even swimming pools were provided. A limit eventually had to be set on the number of tourists visiting a given park, determined usually by the amount of accommodation, which was in turn set by the availability of water. This ceiling has probably been reached in the Kgalagadi Transfrontier Park, yet further camps are planned. Will the underground water hold out? Will rainfall be sufficient to replenish these underground supplies faster than they are tapped? Time will tell whether these camps remain viable.

There are at present seven national parks in the dry western parts of South Africa. They are: Namaqua, Tanqua Karoo, Richtersveld, Augrabies, Karoo, Kalahari Gemsbok, and Mountain Zebra. Together they cover over 1.3 million hectares (or 13 136 square kilometres). This may sound impressive but, given the fragility of the deserts, it may not be enough to conserve all the endemic organisms that live there. However, a balance has to be struck between the areas to be managed and the cost of such management. It is heartening that these national parks are not the only reserves in the dry west of southern Africa and there are several significant conservation areas in Namibia.

In addition to the National Parks there are more than 20 nature reserves in the South African arid west run by provincial or municipal authorities. These vary in size from a few to several hundred hectares; some of them are mainly for recreation, but all provide some natural habitat where visitors may see desert vegetation of different kinds in its natural condition.

The major national parks of Namibia are Etosha, Namib-Naukluft, Skeleton Coast and Fish River Canyon. This last reserve contains the /Ai-/Ais Hot Springs Game Park and together with the Richtersveld it will in time form the Gariep Transfrontier Park with the Orange (or Gariep) River flowing through it.

A huge area in the southwestern part of Namibia stretching from the Orange River to the 26th parallel north of Lüderitz is conceded to De Beers Consolidated Diamond Mines and is designated Diamond Area No. 1, also known by its German name of the *Sperrgebiet*. Not only the actual diamond diggings along the coast, but the whole region is barred to entry by any persons for any purpose whatever, and is therefore in effect a game reserve. Indeed it is in the process of being proclaimed as a protected area or National Park. The former Diamond Area No. 2 stretches as the Namib-Naukluft National Park northward to Swakopmund where it joins up with the Skeleton Coast National Park and runs to the Kunene River, which here forms the border between Namibia and Angola.

Together these three coastal reserves already cover more than 16 000 square kilometres. When they are combined with the Richtersveld to the south, Iona to the north, and the adjacent Huns Mountains and Fish River Canyon complex to the east, they will constitute the largest protected area in Africa – over 73 000 square kilometres. These coastal reserves protect the Namib Desert itself and are therefore of the greatest significance for conservation.

The intrinsic lack of water is likely to keep this region from over-exploitation by development or by inappropriate recreational use, such as irresponsible use of four-wheel-drive vehicles, dune buggies and quad bikes. Especially vulnerable to disturbance is the little Damara Tern, an endemic species that nests on the open flats not far from the coastal beaches.

Has southern Africa addressed its arid-zone conservation priorities adequately? There is no short answer, but the evidence shows that an awareness exists of the importance of this zone for biodiversity. South Africa is recognized as the third most biologically diverse country in the world. If one adds to this the enormous number of endemic organisms in Namibia,

the whole southern African region is of global significance, especially with regard to its Desert and Fynbos biomes. These two biomes merge in the Western Cape, so that the entire west coast of southern Africa from Cape Town to the Kunene River is a biological jewel unsurpassed by any other in the world.

Not only do these reserves protect and conserve the living

Major Conservation Areas

things within them, but they also hold in perpetuity the non-living aspects of the environment – the geology, the landforms, the mineral wealth, the processes of erosion by wind and water, the very air we breathe – all of which contribute to the quality of life on this planet, which is the only one we are ever likely to have.

Mineral riches have attracted people
to the deserts of the world, but
winning them has been difficult
because of the scarcity of water.
Through ingenuity people have often
overcome such problems, but once
the mineral resources have run out
or become unprofitable they have
had to abandon the enterprise. The
desert then takes over again and the
remains of the human endeavours
stand as monuments in the sand,
as here at Kolmanskop on the coast
of Namibia near Lüderitz. Although
mining operations deface a desert
locally, some mining companies help
the cause of conservation by keeping
large areas pristine. Such a major
conservation area is the Sperrgebiet
of Namibia.

Desert places are more accessible today than ever before, but they should not be taken for granted. This amazing environment is worth every effort on the part of individuals and governments to protect it from damage by indiscriminate vehicle tracks, uncontrolled tourism and over-exploitation of underground water.

The solitude of the desert is part of its attraction to humans. The big sky, the spacious landscapes, an absence of other people or human artefacts as far as the eye can see, and the vast silence fill one with an appreciation of one's own smallness in the big scheme of things. One is inspired to marvel anew at the patient endurance of desert plants and animals, and the ways in which they are able to survive and thrive in such an apparently inhospitable environment.

PHOTOGRAPHERS' NOTE

The more stark the landscape, the more intense the sensation of being there. Standing on a deserted rock plain and becoming acutely aware of only the overwhelming heat, silence and dust is somehow more profoundly fulfilling than experiencing an area that is teeming with life. In deserts, loneliness is an almost positive sensation. Perhaps this is because life is taken so much for granted in habitats where animals live on the fast foods of nature. Elsewhere, elephants do not need to walk 80 km for water. Beetles do not have to stand on the top of sand dunes in order to try and condense a drop of drinking water from ethereal mist.

Photographing desert scenes is an experience unequalled in nature photography. Although it is tiring to run after gemsbok on sand dunes or to stalk web-footed geckos or to drive for weeks on rocky roads, the reward is uniquely fulfilling. The harsh conditions do not favour photographers who need to keep dust out of their cameras or who need to survive the sometimes 50-degree Celcius difference between the heat of midday and the severe cold of night. Yet, taking a photograph in a desert is like imbibing a happiness drug and is equally addictive. Every time you press the shutter, it improves your mood. During a single day in the desert a photographer experiences the full range of emotions. From ecstasy at sunrise, to the despair of heat and boredom at midday, to total intoxication at sunset.

It is said that if you sit too long in the shade of a tree in the Kalahari, that a certain kind of blood-sucking mite, called tampan, will climb onto you, attach to your skin, and give you a terrible itch. The same could happen to photographers who are not cautious. If you spend too much time in the desert, something will creep onto you, and get under your skin.

Like it or not.

Heinrich van den Berg
Philip & Ingrid van den Berg

Immature male lion

194

ACKNOWLEDGEMENTS

The Van den Bergs would like to thank the following people: The sponsors, collectors and subscribers who placed their faith in us and helped to make this book possible. Jan and Martha Beukes without whom we could not have managed. Herman and Seugnet van den Berg who are our best critics and supporters. All our friends and family.

   For assistance with promotion and marketing: Mel Cunningham and his staff at Infinity for the efficient way in which they handled the orders from Wild Card members. A special word of appreciation to Hanlie Niemann for her hard work. Ina Michau in Johannesburg, Christi Hattingh in Pietermaritzburg, David McNaughton at Karoo Connections in Graaff-Reinet, Ann Pretorius of the William Humphries Art Gallery in Kimberley, Jaco Powell of Jacals Tours, Morgan Hauptfleisch, Wildlife Resources Manager at De Beers Consolidated Mines. Henriette and Dries Engelbrecht of SANParks, Nico van der Walt, Park Warden at the Kgalagadi Transfrontier Park.

Springbok

For assistance with the photography: Botswana Air for flights to Botswana. The staff of Deception Valley Lodge for their kind hospitality, Susan Rothbletz of Islands in Africa, Riana and Paul Loots, Dr D. Crowe for allowing us to photograph the dinosaur footprints at Sante Sana, Richard Viljoen, as well as Dennet and Rachel Makiin at Sante Sana for their help and hospitality. Herman van den Berg for the use of two of his photographs.

The Macleans wish to acknowledge the following people: Professor Trevor Edwards and Ms Christina Potgieter of the Department of Botany, School of Life Sciences, University of KwaZulu-Natal, Pietermaritzburg, for help with botanical literature. The staff of the Life Sciences Library, University of KwaZulu-Natal, Pietermaritzburg, for help with literature searches. Professor Barry Lovegrove of the Department of Zoology & Entomology, University of KwaZulu-Natal, Pietermaritzburg, for biological advice. Dr Chris Brown, Executive Director, Namibia Nature Foundation, Windhoek, Namibia, for helpful information about existing and proposed conservation measures in Namibia.

SUBSCRIBERS

SPONSORS' EDITION

De Beers Consolidated Mines
Gallo Images
Julian Beth Gosling
Friedrich Krachler
Northern Cape Tourism Authority
Alex Strachan
Harold Tooch
J A (Koos) Vorster

COLLECTORS' EDITION

Michael & Jean Brownie
Pierre Casters
John & Sue Duthie
Jorge Hallak
John K Hepburn
Martin Lampacher
Jean-Pierre & Anne Levy
J D & Edwina Lombard
Pierre Moureau
Ryno Secondo Scribante
The Lehr Family
Ann and Ray Moore
Glenn Anthony Peters
R P Visser
Etienne & Jannet Wolmarans
Dr Allen Zimbler

SPONSORING COMPANIES

Restonic
Tala Private Game Reserve

Standard Edition

Adendorff, Jaco & Karen
Adlam, Hannes & Rika
African Hornbill Safaris
Alziati, Antonio Federico
Amber & James
Andersson, Ingrid
Andrews, Clifford
Angus, Duncan
Ashton, Peter J
Askew, Anne & Brian
Assad, C S
Austen, Neil
Austin, Margie & John
Aylor, Dude
Babbin, Beth
Bacher, I.-Yvette
Badenhorst, Gerda
Badenhorst, Ronél
Bakker, F G
Baldwin, Douglas & Jan
Ball, Rossouw
Bannatyne, Ian & Diane
Barrow, B H
Becker, Anneke
Bekker, Tersia & Schroder, Di
Bellstedt, Dirk & Friederike
Benz, Mathilde
Berger, H M
Bergmann, R F
Berry, Colette & Shaun
Bervoets, Rik
Bester, Chris & Lynn
Bester, Elmi & Rudolf
Bester, Johan & Angela
Bester, Magdalena
Beukes, Prof Gerhard J
Beyer, C N
Bico, Gail
Birkholtz, Linda
Birley, Mands, Cams & Grant
Bischoff, Roland & Sabine
Blanden, Grant L
Blue Elephant Consulting (Pty) Ltd
Blythe-Wood, Colin
Boulle, Nathalie
Bogiages, Greg
Bolton, Michael & Linda
Booysen, Ingrid
Booysen, Willie & Prudensè
Borman, Elsa
Borril, R
Boshoff, De Villiers
Bosman, Marius & Colla
Botes, Fil & Joan
Botes, Jacques
Botha, Charles & Julia
Botha, Fransie & Ria, Ngodwana SA
Botha, Ivan
Botha, Levina
Botha, Steven & Elaine
Bothma, Rachel C
Botts, E R
Boulton, Dennis
Bouwer, Jan
Brain, Stephen
Braithwaite, Glenda & Jai

Brake, Richard L
Braude, Mike
Brebner, Hamish & Jenny
Breedt, Johannes, Elain, Robert & Melani
Briffa, F
Brits, Kobie
Bromilow, Gavin & Rose
Broom, Judy & Derek
Browne, Anne & Michael
Buchanan, Molly
Buckton, Dr Sally Erika
Bullen, Karen & Gerald
Burger, Ferdie
Burger, Reitz
Burgess, Jillian & Craig Buchan
Bwana, Mitch
Calder, Dr John & Brenda

Caraluchs
Cartier-Nillon, Julien
Cass, Henry & Twinks
Cassel, Graham
Cassel, Max
Cater, John & Mandy
Chait, Laurence
Cheesman, Brenda & Peter
Cheng Yeow Leong
Childes, Michael
Clarence, B G
Clark Family, Northriding Estates
Clark, Bev & Jeremy
Clunnie, Gavin & Rhu
Cockbain, Ian
Coetzee, Ben
Coetzee, Louis
Cohen, Derek
Cole Family
Comber, Lance
Comley, Derrick & Leonie

Conrad, Fred & Muriel
Conradie, Francois D
Cooke, Campbell & Cheryl
Cooke, Duncan & Inès
Corbett, Gareth Cameron
Cornelius, Lampies & Leisha
Crafford, I B
Cronjé, Elmarié
Cross, Ant
Cugno, Diego (Digs)
Damelin, Beverley, Tony & Chani
Daniel, P M
Darroll, Peter & Sue
Davidson, Christo & Martha
Davidson, Lara & Colin
Davison, John – Wildlife Experiences
De Beer, Charles Frederick
De Beer, Hardie & Leonora
De Beers Consolidated Mines
De Beyer, David L
De Castro, Jose, Brenda, Daniela, Michelle

De Graaf, Perry
De Klerk, Carys, Ang & Chris
De Kock, Joan
De Villiers, André
De Villiers, J J
De Villiers, Reenen
De Voogt, W R
De Vries, Gerda & Jan
De Wet, John
Deere, Peter
Den Hartog
Denil, R F J
Dennill, Michael Ingrid Gabriella Rafaela
Dewes Family
Dicker, Mel
Doepel, W R
Dorfan, J
Dott, Graeme
Draycon, Paula & Marie Petit
Dreyer, Kobus & Kate Donaldson
Du Plessis, Enid

Du Plessis, J D
Du Plessis, Jan & Thalita
Du Plessis, Koot
Du Plessis, Pieter G
Du Plessis, Soretha
Du Plooy, T L
Du Preez, Etienne
Du Preez, Johan
Du Preez, Johann & Marie – Nelspruit
Du Toit, Frik & Corrie
Du Toit, Nick & Helga
Ducray, Aileen & Claudia Stocken
Eales, Fiona
Earnshaw, Geoff & Elise
Earnshaw, Jason & Jenny
Edelstein, Alan & Belinda
Edkins, Graham
Edmonds, Mrs M G
Ehlers, Ilse & Dieter
Ellis, Purdon
Ellis-Mattisson, Helen

Elphick, Howard & Laura Pozniak
Engelbrecht, Angel
English, David J
Enslin, Dr Freddie
Erasmus, Fanie
Esterhuyse, Abraham
Ewertse, Anthony & Desiree
Fahrenheim, P D
Fairon, Gavin & Mary
Fairon, Michael
Faul, Alfred & Alta
Faul, Anthony
Faul, Buks
Felizardo, Joao & Gena
Fell, Janet
Fernandes, S
Ferreira, Deon
Fewell, Kate
Field, Alan & Ursula
Findlay, Grant & Lee
Fischer, Tina & Otto

Fitzgerald, Shane
Fletcher, Vernon & Marí
Flückiger, M & W
Forker, Nicole
Fourie, André & Danita
Fourie, H
Fourie, Jan H – Randburg
Fourie, Johan en Magda – VDBPark
Fourie, Leon
Franck, S A
Frandsen, Robin
Fraser, Colin Hugh
Frazer, Mr & Mrs D
Frei, René & Annelies
Friederich, Reinhard & Yvonne
Friedman, Russel, Bonnie & Gabriella
Friemelt, E W L
Frost, Pam & Howard
Garland, Louísa
Gebhardt, Annemarie – WCED
Gemmell, D & R
Gerber, Peet & Madeleine
Gerner, Otto
Geyer, Hardus & Martie
Gibbs, Chris & Lisa
Giblin, Maura
Gilbert, Dixie
Gilliam, Ian
Gillings, Greg
Goater, Christine & Terry
Gobabeb Training & Research Centre
Goodall, S
Gouws, Shirley & Mark
Gray, Peter
Greenaway, Kyle & Kerry
Gresse, Magriet
Greyling, Dr J A (Koos)
Griffioen, Johan
Grobbelaar, Elionora
Grobbelaar, Neil
Grobbelaar, Nick & Leonora
Grobbelaar, Nico & Gesin
Grobler, D C
Grobler, E F
Grobler, J A
Grobler, P & J
Grobler, Piet & Isabella
Grundling, Una & Louis Pieterse
Grundy, Sharon & John
Gubic, Kristina
Günther, Hesma M
Haasbroek, George & Elma
Haffejee, Ismail Abass
Hagemann, Pat & Basil
Hagerman, R K (Dickie)
Hagerman, Richard
Hain, Stuart & Margaret
Hammond, Dr Christopher A
Hammond, Wayne
Hansen, Cuan
Hansen, Len & Mariette
Hardy, Herbert Ernest 'Ian'
Harris, Marilyn & John
Havenga, B M
Heitzer Family
Hellberg, Pam & Berti
Helms, Charles
Henchel, Dr Jon
Henschel, H
Henderson, Rob

Suricate

Hendry, Tony & Bernadette
Hennig, J J – Montagu
Henning, Des & Linda
Henning, Miekie & Pieter
Heinsohn, I
Hepburn, John K
Herrick, Bruce W
Herbert, Cheryl
Hersov, Basil
Hesse Familie
Heyns, Johan & Sue
Hickman, Brett, Liz, James & Cameron
Hilder, C C
Hind, Craig & Caroline
Hirst Family
Holley, Tyrena L
Honiball, Lorraine
Hood, Diana
Hoogervorst, Arend
Hooker, Audrey & Owen
Hopkins & Peach
Horstmann, Peter Intloko Ye Ndlovu
Horvitch, Martin W
Horwitz, M N
Hulett, Peter
Hulse, Mike & Jan
Human, Desmond
Human, P G
Human, Sandy
Jackaman, Wayne & Monica
Jacobs, Gert & Christelle
Jacobs, W H
Jager, Ger & Ineke
James, Rodney & Chantel
James, Tim & Teresa
Jarratt, Tony & Maureen
Johnston, R B & M P
Jones, Dorothy & Mike
Joos, Kevin
Jooste, J A
Jordaan, J A G
Joubert, Anne-Mari & Wessel
Joubert, Jozua, Elize & Elanie
Kaiser, Karl & Loraine
Kalden, Gerhard & Gitta
Karrim, Hajera
Kathrada, Ahmed & Riaz – Waterside
Katz, Kaj William
Keawprasit, Jaruwan
Keeble, R F
Kelfkens, Ian
Kellett, Jeremy & Rina
Kendrick, African Bush Lodge, Marloth Park
Keys, Eddie & Sylvia
Keyser, Volkmar & Claire
Kiblböck, Georg Ludwig
Kihn, Clive M
Kilchenmann, Margrit & Marcel
Kincaid-Smith, Christine
Kindsvogel, Astrid
King, Professor Laetitia
Kirsten, Louis en Liesl
Kirsten, Milton
Kitching, Eugene
Klagsbrun Family
Klinge, F T & Family
Kloppers, F C
Kneale, Clive & Denise
Knight, Joan
Knott, David & Noleen

Koorts Familie
Kotzé, Huibrecht
Kotze, J L
Kotze, Sarel, Mollie & Jaco
Kotzé, Wicus & Marietjie
Kownatzki, Klaus-Peter
Krantz, Edrich
Kraut, Colin & Meredith
Kretschmer, David & Deidre
Kriek, Derik
Kritzinger, Jurie
Krone, Franci & Mariaan
Kruger, Deon
Kruger, Dr Freddie, Teresa & Kids
Kruger, E C
Kruger, Jan
Krüger, Walda Almien
Kruger, Wilhelm & Gesin
Krugler-Felsch, Karin
Kruip, Jochen
Kuipers, M C
Kumaranayagam, S
Kwezi V3 Engineers
Labuschagne, Ben & Elaine
Labuschagne, Hans
Lagaay, Joy
Laserson, Marian & Jack
Laubscher, Andrew, Annemarie & Sons
Lauritzen, R S
Lavoipierre, Alain
Le Sueur, Mr & Mrs
Leger, Yolanda & Daniel
Lellyett, Gavin, Janet, Bianca & Claire
Lewis, S S E
Liatos, George, Barbara & Gaughan
Liebenberg, Dantes
Lloyd-Townsend, Adolf
Lloyd, Rodney & Family
Lombard, Bregda
Lønborg-Madsen, Eva
Lorber, Franz
Loreggian, Eddie
Loubser, J
Loubser, Johann D
Lourens, Frans
Louw, M J o
Louw, Susan
Louw, Wynand & Wiana
Luck, Robert & Gillian
Ludin, Esther
Lukes, Jackie
Lukes, Tim & Monica
Lurie, Ruth
Luz, Walter – Weltevreden Park Ext 26
Maasch, Carol
MacFarlane, Mark Reid
MacGillicuddy, Jaco
Machado, Ricardo
MacKenzie, Craig & Lynn
Mackenzie, O J
Mackey, Jon
MacQuilkan, Peter; Managa Hills Magalies
Main, Tom
Makings, Kevin & Barbara
Mallon, Godfrey
Maloney, Cynthia & Shane
Mance, Beefy
Marais, D D
Marais, Hans & Engela
Marshall, David Reuben

Marais, Mornay & Magda – Nelspruit
Maria, Emanuel
Martin, Richard
Martin, Rob & Andre
Marx, Johan
Mayer, Quirin
McCalgan, Sam & Mark
McCourt, Gayle & Colin
McCreadie, Alfred Hugo
McDonald, Cindy
McDonald, Denis & René
McDonald, Neil
McGinn, Helen
McIntosh, Candace E
McKenzie, N W
McLeod, D J
Meadows, John & Trish
Mearns, Kevin, Martie & Enrique
Meiring, Pieter
Meunier, Stephane
Miller, Marna & Billy
Middleton, G O
Minnaar, Derek
Minnie, Matt & Chrisna
Mitchell, Anthony Kerr
Mitchell, Lily & Duncan
Mollentze, Nadia & Rhuan
Möller, Charl
Moore, Carole A
Moore, Charles W
Morant, Patrick
Morford, Dr Rippon & Mrs Margot
Morley B
Morley, Ashley & Linda
Morris, Les, Eva & Sean
Morris, M
Morrison, Bruce, Sharon, Brett & Nicole
Morton, Lex & Jill
Moseley, Ronnie
Mostert J
Muller, Charlie & Angela Steele
Muller, Vanessa
Myburg, Alta
Namdeb Diamond Corporation
Namib Lodge Company
Napier, Richard
Naude, C
Neal, Mr T R
Nel, Ds George
Nel, H S K
Nel, Johann & Ina
Nel, Len en Jacqueline
Nel, Phillip & Annelise
Nel, Peet
Newton-Perry, Alan
Niemand, Hennie & Tootje
Nieuwoudt, Marius
Nogueira, Antonio Joao Martins
Noome, Idette & Chris
Oberholzer, Ds Christo & Thea
O'Connor, Cedric & Judy
Odendaal, Adriaan & Sandra
Oertel, James
Ogilvie-Thompson, T
Oldenburger, Han
Oosthuizen, Brian & Ruby
Oosthuizen, Carel & Hilda, Addo
Oosthuizen, Coenraad, Adele & Seuns
Oosthuizen, Gavin & Angela
Oosthuizen, Pieter & Corlia

Oosthuysen, Herman & Christelle
Opperman, Lida
Osborn, Pamela Lorraine
Oudmayer, Jurriaan
Outhwaite, Pat
Outram, Deirdre & Ian
Ovendale, Dr & Mrs C O
Pablos-Ruiz, Carlos
Pais, Rina
Palmer, Graham
Parnell, Owen
Parsley, Jeff & Bev
Paterson, Angus & Sharon
Patrick, Colin & Glynnis
Paul, N J L
Payne, Barry
Payne, J P & Debbie
Peddie, Graham S
Penrith, William
Perrins, Debbie & Niall
Peters, Allan Francis
Peters, Dennis
Peters, Glenn A & Gary Van Eyk (Inyatsi)
Peters, Lyle
Peters, Seth Alaric
Petersen, Clive
Petyt, Trent
Phatudi, Tebogo & Team
Pheiffer, L M
Phillips, Avril Elaine
Pienaar, Danie & Susan
Pienaar, Jacus
Pieterse, Bertie
Pieterse, Tinus & Joey
Plastow, Michael – Earth & Sky
Podmore, Kevin, Glynis & Family
Polich, Carol
Porter, Michael, Kim, Chobe & Sabie
Potgieter, Brad & Bridgitte
Potgieter, Derick
Potter, Kevin & Tania
Pound, Dudley Sidney
Pretorius, Elma
Pretorius, Eugene
Priem, J
Prinsloo, Hennie
Prinsloo, Louw & Annalie
Prozesky, Julienne
Prozesky, Max & Lylah
Quanjer, Arnoud
Quanjer, Duco
Rademan, C F
Ramotebele, Lesiba Standford
Ramsay Engineering (Pty) Ltd
Ranger, Michael & Mersa
Ray, Amit
Read, David & Diane
Reid, Sonia
Reinhardt, Errol
Reuter, Helmuth & Ulrike Reuter
Ridge, Simon & Lee
Ritchie, Neil
Robb, Malcolm & Glenda
Robertson, Cliff & Christina
Robinson, Bruce
Rod, Alec
Roelandts-Verbeke, Nathalie
Rogers, Richard
Rohrmann, Juergen
Roodbol Rudy, Brenda, Rebert, Marnus

Roods, Ian & Merja
Rosenmeyer, Walter Hermann
Rossouw, Pierre
Rothrock, Steve
Roulet, G A
Routledge, Sean Kennedy
Ruf, Tanja
Rüfenacht, Heidy & Heinz
Rumpf, Dirk
Ryder, Marc & Lorna
Rynhoud, Mark
Salijee, Hanifa Ahmed
Sampson, Alan
Samson Family

Ground Squirrel

Taback, Mark Julian
Tasioulas Family
Taylor Paul & Zelda
Taylor, Ernie T
Tellabs SA (Pty) Ltd.
Tennant, Professor & Mrs P M W
Terblanche, H M & E
Terblanche, Samuel
The Hidden Family
Theron, Wiaan
Thompson, Gerald Bryan
Thompson, Hugh
Thorpe, Bradley
Toms, Nic, Megz, Emma & Shelly
Tours Unlimited
Towell, Chris & John
Treasure, John & Joan
Tree M & M
Trendler, Roy
Trollope, Winston S W
Truter, Kristo & Tita
Turnbull, Peter G
TWP Consulting (Pty) Ltd
University of KwaZulu-Natal, Pmb
Van Coller, Hendrik & Marietjie
Van de Wetering, Ard & Marissa
Van de Wetering, Klaas en Rietje
Van den Berg, Alta
Van den Berg, André & Gwen
Van den Berg, Carmen
Van den Berg, Herman & Seugnet
Van den Berg, Tom & Trix
Van der Eecken, Kerner J
Van der Jagt, Dick & Liz
Van der Merwe, D A
Van der Merwe, Dr Roelof
Van der Merwe, Gerhard
Van der Merwe, Paul J
Van der Merwe, T
Van der Merwe, Thys
Van der Ryst, Elna & Louna
Van der Schyff, B
Van der Schyff, Henry & Connie
Van der Westhuizen, Ben
Van der Westhuizen, J J & Debbie
Van der Westhuizen, Magdel & Attie
Van der Westhuizen, Sean & Heidi
Van der Windt, Fred
Van Dyk, Sybrand & Wilma
Van Essen, L E
Van Graan, Ivan & Marilyn
Van Heerden, Colette & Marc
Van Huyssteen, R Z I
Van Heerden, Sakkie
Van Jaarsveld, Keegan
Van Loggerenberg, D E
Van Loon, Louis
Van Niekerk, Chris
Van Niekerk, Christina
Van Niekerk, Kanah E
Van Niekerk, Sonja
Van Noord, Peter
Van Rensburg, Dudley
Van Rensburg, Lena
Van Rooy, Louis
Van Rooyen, Pierre
Van Santen, Neil
Van Schalkwyk, A
Van Vuuren, Lynn
Van Waardenburg, Denice

Van Wyk, Christina Elizabeth
Van Wyk, Johan – Swaziland
Van Wyk, Leon, Christine & Francois
Van Zyl, A G
Van Zyl, J A
Van Zyl, Jif & Celia
Van Zyl, Johan
Van Zyl, Leon
Van Zyl, Oma Meta
Varanini Family
Vemer, Coen & Lous
Vemer, Eric & Kari
Venter, Elzabé
Venter, Hester en Boet
Venter, Pieter J
Verwoerdt, Ari & Marlene
Viljoen, H W
Vine, Peta
Vine, Simon
Visser, Giel & Lucille
Visser, Nico
Viviers, Freek
Volman, Hans & Christa
Von Memerty, P W
Von Willich, Willem & Sandra
Vosloo, Rita & Barry, Jeffreys Bay
Vos-Paulides, Herry & Jeannette
Voutsas, G & Family
Wackrill, G D
Wallace, Jeni & Bruce
Ward-Christian, Ivan & Joanna
Warrington, J H
Watchurst, Gavin
Watson, T
Wearing, Craig & Ursula
Weaving, Alan
Webber, John & Jennifer
Weedon, Odyle & Anthony
Weight, James & Jean
Wessels & Hattingh Ing/Inc
Wessels H J
West, Ethan Joaquin
Westwood, Dave
White, John
Wiese, Dirk Jr
Wiese, Ingrid & Stefan
Willemse, Hannes
Williams, Carole
Willoughby, Rodney & Noleen
Winchester, Tarryn Lee
Winterbottom, Matthew Anthony
Wiseman, Chris & Peta
Woessner, C
Wolmarans, Etienne & Jannet
Wolstenholme, B Nigel
Woolley, Bryn
Wörsdörfer, Saliem
Woudstra, F S
Wright, Darryl & Cibotto Giovanna
Wright, Michael & Dawn
Wylie, Dan
Yammin, M D
Young, Jayne F
Yssel, Frik en Therese
Zaczek, Ulrike
Zarrabi, Eppie
Zahnd, Brigitte & Patrick
Zietsman, Derek – Wildlife Artist
Zietsman, Paula
Zimmer, Wolfgang M

Bushveld Elephant Shrew

Selected Bibliography

Adams, Jill. 1976. *Wild flowers of the Northern Cape.* Cape Town, South Africa: Department of Nature & Environmental Conservation of the Provincial Administration of the Cape of Good Hope.

Craven, Patricia & Marais, Christine. 1986. *Namib flora: Swakopmund to the Giant Welwitschia via Goanikontes.* Windhoek, Namibia: Gamsberg Macmillan.

Bornman, Chris H. 1978. *Welwitschia: paradox of a parched paradise.* Cape Town, South Africa: Struik.

Branch, Bill. 1988. Field guide to the snakes and other reptiles of southern Africa. Cape Town, South Africa: Struik.

Broadley, Donald G. 1983. *FitzSimons' snakes of southern Africa.* Johannesburg, South Africa: Delta Books.

Dorst, Jean & Dandelot, Pierre. 1970. *A field guide to the larger mammals of Africa.* London: Collins.

Fearn, Jacqueline. 1980. *Discovering heraldry.* Aylesbury, United Kingdom: Shire Publications.

Hall-Martin, Anthony & Carruthers, Jane (Eds). 2003. *South African National Parks: a celebration.* Auckland Park, South Africa: Horst Klemm.

Le Roux, A. & Schelpe, E.A.C.L.E. 1981. *South African Wild Flower Guide 1: Namaqualand and Clanwilliam.* Cape Town, South Africa: Botanical Society of South Africa and Cape Department of Nature & Environmental Conservation.

Lovegrove, Barry. 1993. *The living deserts of southern Africa.* Vlaeberg, South Africa: Fernwood Press.

Louw, Gideon & Seely, Mary. 1982. *Ecology of desert organisms.* London: Longman.

Maclean, Gordon Lindsay. 1993. *Roberts' birds of southern Africa.* (Sixth Edition), Cape Town, South Africa: Trustees of the John Voelcker Bird Book Fund.

Maclean, Gordon Lindsay. 1990. *Ornithology for Africa.* Pietermaritzburg, South Africa: University of Natal Press.

Maclean, Gordon Lindsay. 1996. *Ecophysiology of desert birds.* Berlin: Springer-Verlag.

Main, Mike & Fowkes, John & Sandra. 1987. *Visitors' guide to Botswana: how to get there, what to see, where to stay.* Johannesburg, South Africa: Southern.

Manning, John & Paterson-Jones, Colin. 2004. *Southern African wild flowers: jewels of the veld.* Cape Town, South Africa: Struik.

Nussey, Wilf. 1993. *The crowded desert: the Kalahari Gemsbok National Park.* Rivonia, South Africa: William Waterman.

Dictionary Unit for South African English. 1996. *A dictionary of South African English on historical principles.* New York: Oxford University Press.

Reader's Digest. 1978. *Illustrated guide to southern Africa.* Cape Town, South Africa: Reader's Digest.

Seely, Mary. 1992. *The Namib: natural history of an ancient desert.* (Second Edition), Windhoek, Namibia: Shell Namibia Ltd.

Brant's Whistling Rat

Shearing, David & van Heerden, Katryn. 1994. *South African wild flower guide 6: Karoo.* Kirstenbosch, South Africa: Botanical Society of South Africa & National Botanical Institute.

Smithers, Reay H. N. 1983. *The mammals of the southern African subregion.* Pretoria, South Africa: University of Pretoria.

Stuart, Chris & Tilde. 1988. *Field guide to the mammals of southern Africa.* Cape Town, South Africa: Struik.

Swaney, Deanna. 2002. *Namibia.* Melbourne, Australia: Lonely Planet.

Tobias, Phillip V. (Ed.) 1978. *The Bushmen: San hunters and herders of southern Africa.* Cape Town, South Africa: Human & Rousseau.

Van der Walt, Pieter. 2000. *Augrabies splendour: a guide to the natural history of the Augrabies Falls National Park and the Riemvasmaak wildlife area.* Pretoria, South Africa: Info Naturae.

Williamson, Graham. 2000. *Richtersveld: the enchanted wilderness.* Hatfield, South Africa: Umdaus Press.

Willis, J.C. 1957. *A dictionary of the flowering plants and ferns.* Cambridge, U.K.: Cambridge University Press.

Copyright © 2005 by **HPH Publishing**

Standard Edition

ISBN 0-620-34343-5

Collectors' Edition

ISBN 0-620-34345-1

Sponsors' Edition

ISBN 0-620-34344-3

Photography by **HPH Photography**

Heinrich van den Berg

Philip & Ingrid van den Berg

Text by Gordon & Cherie Maclean

Maps by Hanlie Volman

Edited by John Deane

Proofread by Valda Strauss

Design, typesetting and reproduction by

Heinrich van den Berg, **HPH Publishing**

Printed and bound in Singapore by

Tien Wah Press (Pte.) Ltd

Published by **HPH Publishing**

First edition, first impression 2005

P.O.Box 13244, Cascades, 3202, South Africa

Email: info@hphpublishing.co.za

Website: www.hphpublishing.co.za

Captions for following pages:

1. Black-maned lion – Kgalagadi Transfrontier Park

2-3 Namaqua Chameleon – Namib Desert

4-5 African Elephant – Purros, Kaokoland

6-7 Dune 45 – Near Sossusvlei

8-9 Mountain Desert – Richtersveld

10-11 Juvenile Pale Chanting Goshawk – Kgalagadi Transfrontier Park

12-13 Klipspringer – Augrabies Falls National Park

14-15 Sandstorm – Sossusvlei

24-25 Web-footed Gecko – Namib Desert

68-69 Namaqua Chameleon – Damaraland

100-101 Eastern Cape Crag Lizard – Valley of Desolation

132-133 Male Ground Agama – Kgalagadi Transfrontier Park

186-187 Barking Gecko – Kgalagadi Transfrontier Park

208 Suricate family – Kgalagadi Transfrontier Park